My Chernobyl

The Human Story of a Scientist and the
Nuclear Power Plant Catastrophe

Alexander A. Borovoi

Translated by Julya Borovoi
Foreword by Gary Dunbar

My Chernobyl
Copyright 2017 by Alexander Borovoi
Foreword Copyright 2017 by Gary Dunbar

All rights reserved. Please do not reproduce or distribute without express written permission of the author.

Published by Piscataqua Press
142 Fleet St., Portsmouth, NH 03801
www.ppressbooks.com
info@piscataquapress.com

ISBN: 978-1-944393-72-4

Explanation of the back cover photo:

Scientists, limited to a maximum five-minute search, were lowered into dangerously high-radiation parts of the destroyed reactor to determine the amount of nuclear fuel that might have been buried beneath the materials that were dropped from helicopters in an attempt to contain the radiation.

Contents

Foreword i
Prelude 1
1. Chernobyl 1
2. Gravity of First Decisions 9
3. Where Are the Thrown Materials? 16
4. Teachers 21
5. My Mother 29

Chernobyl — 1986 35
1. First Steps 37
2. Some Words About My Work and Everyday Life 42
3. Shelter 50
4. The Precepts 54
5. Robots 64
6. Great Building 71
7. Two Hours 79
8. Apples 86

1987 and Further 91
1. When I Began to Write This Book 93
2. Elephant Leg 96
3. Books and Photos 105
4. October 13, 1987 114
5. Seven Days in May 123

The Final Chapter 129
Conclusion—2017 135
Afterword 145
About the Author 149

And the name of the star is called Wormwood: and the third part of the waters became wormwood; and many men died of the waters, because they were made bitter.

—The Revelation of St. John 8:11 (King James Version)

Chernobyl is a sort of wormwood in Ukraine.

Foreword

The Chernobyl accident in 1986, the only explosion of a nuclear power plant to date, is worthy of a special place in human memory for the number of critically important lessons learned. Alexander A. Borovoi's twenty-three years of work at Chernobyl provide insight into the panic, confusion, missteps, heroism, and, finally, critical clear-headed analysis and scientific thinking that enabled the effective resolution of the Chernobyl catastrophe.

In August 2001, *U.S. News and World Report* included Borovoi in its list of twenty living "real heroes." That recognition was the direct result of his finding order in the midst of chaos at Chernobyl. Through Borovoi and those he worked with, we see how some humans' behavior in a catastrophe can be well-meaning but ineffective; while others, through knowledge, discipline, and sacrifice, bring events under control and put them on track to ultimate resolution. The deceptively simple lesson of his book—that panic will not resolve a catastrophe and may make it worse—certainly applies to nuclear-energy facilities, but it is also critical to our response to the increasing impacts of climate and weather change; large releases or explosions of hazardous materials; potential collisions with a meteor, comet, or asteroid; eruptions of massive volcanos, such as the overdue one in Yellowstone Park; and other potential global catastrophe.

When the Chernobyl accident occurred, no plans or procedures existed for such an event. This oversight resulted in the failure to quickly comprehend the magnitude and

Alexender A. Borovoi

nature of the accident, and allowed for the hasty implementation of responses that either made the accident worse, such as in the loss of lives; or the well-meaning efforts that interfered with one another and slowed the progress of effective responses. The pathway out of this state of confusion was difficult and took time. This was the path that Borovoi created.

He was born in Moscow and has lived there all his life, except for the twenty-three years when he worked at Chernobyl. He is a family man with a wife, Tamila, two sons, grandchildren, and great-grandchildren.

He graduated from Moscow Engineering Physics Institute in 1962 and entered the Kurchatov Institute as a young engineer. From there he progressed to Senior Research Associate, to Candidate, and finally to Doctor of Nuclear Physics. He cooperated and exchanged ideas with the "great generation"—A. P. Alexandrov, S. T. Belyaev, I. K. Kikoin, Y. A. Smorodinsky, G. N. Flerov, and many others. He created the neutrino-physics laboratory at the second reactor of the Rivne Nuclear Power Plant, where he also developed the neutrino detector.

In addition to his academic diplomas, Russia honored him with the award "For Courage" and the State award, and a rank of the "honored worker in science and technology." *New World* magazine identified his book, *My Chernobyl*, published in 1996, as the best work in journalism in that year.

The Chernobyl accident pulled Borovoi, and thousands of others, into pandemonium. While some moved on to create safer designs for nuclear power plants or better ways to train the operators, Borovoi's focus for those twenty-three years was the recovery from the accident. He continues that work today at the Kurchatov Institute.

My Chernobyl

I met Borovoi at Chernobyl in August 1991 during a trip to Kiev, Ukraine, at the invitation of the organization that would eventually become the ministry responsible for addressing the aftermath of the Chernobyl accident. That trip launched for me a decade of work in Ukraine, Belarus, and Russia, a decade that taught me many lessons about the differences in the complexities of American and Russian cultures, and why we have difficulties understanding each other. The exception to those difficulties is the creation of deep friendships. That decade gave me the gift of friendship with Borovoi and his wife.

Borovoi's achievements made my work possible. My task was to help the Ministry of Ukraine for Protection of the Population from the Consequences of the Chernobyl Nuclear Plant Accident. My specific task was preparing a master plan summary of the ministry's mission, for presentation to the European Bank for Reconstruction and Development. This summary, by an American, was necessary because of the enormous gap between bureaucratic and cultural practices of Western institutions and Soviet government structures. In January 1992, I delivered a fifty-three-page four-phase master plan, defining each task, the results to be achieved, and the estimated costs in both grant and debt financing. The total estimated cost of the first three phases was $352,080,000.00. If Borovoi had not been successful in caging that initial chaos at Chernobyl, it would have been impossible to even consider starting a master plan.

I would like to say that my effort unlocked a flow of the money that was necessary to address the Chernobyl accident. That, I cannot claim. However, my work did help the international discussion move forward and find the path that led to construction of the structure that now encloses both the destroyed reactor and the sarcophagus that was built in an

Alexender A. Borovoi

earlier attempt to contain it. The New Safe Confinement (NSC) structure was rolled into place in 2016 and will be fully operational by the end of 2017.

After Borovoi and I had gotten to know each other, he traveled to the United States to make numerous presentations of technical information on the Chernobyl accident, and he frequently stayed at our home. He told me that when he heard me speak Russian, he knew he had to learn English. My Russian is terrible, but what is amazing is the method Borovoi used to learn English. He taught himself one word each day. Not just the word, but everything about it: spelling, use, grammar, origin, and the other mysteries of the English language. After his first year of learning, we had lengthy conversations. After the second, we could collaborate on and solve problems. After the third, Borovoi stood at the podium for major gatherings, presenting the Chernobyl story and taking questions from American audiences in many cities across this country.

In this book, he writes about some of the people he worked with and some of the events—alternately comic and terrifying—that occurred in the first years he was at Chernobyl. As one learns more of his story, it becomes obvious that the problem of the Chernobyl catastrophe, and of many other catastrophes, is how the panic of an initial response can cloud and obfuscate critical information. Controlling that panic and rectifying its attendant problems was Borovoi's signature achievement and key to resolving the Chernobyl crisis.

—Gary Dunbar

Prelude

1. Chernobyl

Rocket, a small boat on submarine wings, left the quay and went upstream the River Dnieper. It was a warm, sunny day, and the churches and monasteries on the right bank could be clearly seen. The benches on Rocket were covered with white material and polyethylene.

Almost at once, everyone started to put on the clothes they'd been given before boarding: thick socks, white "soldier" underwear, khaki working suits. Everybody was also given two shallow envelopes. Inside were *lepestok*—petals—lightweight respirators. The lepestok covered noses and mouths with a special fabric called Petryanov's fabric, or filter, on behalf of its inventor. One needs good instructions or a good example to put the lepestok on properly. Otherwise, you are sure to put it on incorrectly, and the safety of your breathing will exist only in your mind. Nobody, of course, gave us any instructions, and we put on our respirators as best we could.

I couldn't use them properly for a very long time, and when I learned at last, I tried to teach others dozens, hundreds, of times. Especially young soldiers, who were knocking down radioactive concrete dust with pick hammers. Two years later, when a continuous war with plutonium dust started inside the destroyed Unit 4, I was skilled enough to discuss our needs with the famous Academician Petryanov, inventor of this fabric. He even presented me his book with a dedicatory inscription.

We put our clothes on and sat almost without talking. When we did talk, we whispered.

Alexender A. Borovoi

Rocket came to the mouth of the River Pripyat, passing the tied vessels that were used as living space for workers, and reached the quay.

"Welcome to Chernobyl!" was announced from the captain's bridge (fig. 1).

Figure 1. The destroyed block, May 1986

My Chernobyl

Everybody has his own Chernobyl. Millions of human lives were sucked into the whirlpool of this tragedy, and every life was refracted and distorted. I haven't the slightest idea how the other people involved will understand and interpret my refraction of Chernobyl. But the everlasting human wish to share experience and knowledge, to boast—you may call this whatever you like—this human wish, which grows in the course of time with the approach of the zone of eternal silence, gives me no peace. I'm always going over different moments, which seem to be really interesting, in my mind, trying to put them together, like stacking bricks. Some events have many witnesses; some have no witnesses but me.

* * *

"Our dosimeters can't display more than 200 roentgens per hour,"[1] I am saying. "Maybe there are about 2000? How can we get out of this situation?"

"By using your own senses!"

"But a man doesn't feel radiation. Even in our books and in lectures, they say that radiation has no color, no smell, no taste."

"This is only in lectures. The lecturers have been staying in Moscow and can't reach Chernobyl. High radiation fields have a smell. And if you smell this, don't display any heroism, but quickly—quickly—reel your fishing lines in and run away as quickly as you can."

---

[1] Radiation is measured in roentgens, in honor of the German physicist Wilhelm Röntgen. It is expressed in units of one hour; 1R/h is equal to an external dose of one roentgen in one hour. If a body receives a uniform dose of radiation that measures 300–500 R/h, death occurs in 50% of cases, due to injury to bone marrow.

Alexender A. Borovoi

"What is the smell?"

"Ozone. The first precept: be afraid of the smell of ozone."

* * *

It's autumn. Boris Scherbina, the Chairman of the Government Commission—we called him Chairman—and Academician Legasov are in Scherbina's office on the second floor. Some minutes ago, Legasov came into our headquarters—a small room with three tables—and brought me to the Chairman. The Chairman does not waste time on introductions.

"Do you know that radiation above the Unit increased by four times?" he says. "Didn't know yet? Pilots of the helicopters registered this fact today. And your physicists registered temperature increases in the lower rooms, under the exploded reactor. Why nobody reported the fact to me immediately, we will find out later. We have no time now. The activity of air filters around the Unit increased by dozens of times.

"It seems that an uncontrollable chain nuclear reaction has started inside the Unit. You are to learn the reason. Quickly and thoroughly. I can give you only two hours. If you cannot prove that this is not a nuclear hazard, we will raise the alarm and lead the people out of the plant. Thousands of people are working there today. I can't give you more time.

"Until you fulfill the task and report personally to me or Academician Legasov, you shouldn't talk about nuclear hazard. It is usual staff work. Urgent work, but a usual one. Any help will be rendered immediately."

I return to the headquarters. An unknown man follows me. He shows me his documents; he is an officer of the Committee of State Security (KGB). He tells me insistently to sign every piece of paper, every list of calculations, and then to give everything to him. Again and again, he warns me of responsibility.

* * *

I'm sitting inside the Unit. Light fades. The situation is not new—the workers have chopped the power cable again. Everyone is in a great hurry. The holidays are coming, and we are to finish building "Shelter"—a construction that will cover the destroyed Unit 4 so that rains and winds will not spread radioactivity out of the Unit. The level of radioactivity is so high in some places, human life can be measured only in minutes. If you stay there for a minute or two, you may never come back.

The light is switched off, but we have miner's torches; and in their beams I see a good but absent-minded fellow near me. He was to accompany a photographer, who had just arrived from Moscow, to take some photos of "Elephant Leg," a big radioactive stalactite that was found by explorers in one of the reactor's lower rooms. The room is dark, but it is lighted enough that I would notice the photographer. He is not there.

"What have you managed to photograph?" I ask cautiously.

In the light of the torches, I can see the man's face growing absolutely pale, even white.

"I led him," he says, "to the room on the right ... returned to others, and forgot, quite forgot, that he is there ... below. He is waiting, can't get out himself..."

* * *

Alexender A. Borovoi

At the daily briefing, I say, "Tomorrow we have to visit one interesting but unpleasant place. Can we reach it?"

"You needn't go there. The fellows have just visited it. And took some photos, switched on an alarm counter."

"What fellows? What damned fellows? Who allowed them? In such high radioactive fields!"

"Fellows. Well, Kolya ... and me."

* * *

An article in a newspaper. "These people are climbing inside the Unit only for one reason—for getting high salaries."

* * *

And again the office of Valery Legasov comes back to my memory. Legasov: an Academician, Member of Government Commission, Vice Director of one of the most famous institutes in Russia, the Kurchatov Institute (fig. 2).

The office is empty. Some days ago Legasov committed suicide. I was asked to check his papers and belongings for radioactivity before giving them to his family. They are lying on his table, covered with polyethylene.

I read somewhere that all of Pierre and Marie Curie's belongings in the Curie Museum in Paris are radioactive. If you level your counter to them, it will start tapping, and this will last practically forever.

I level my counter to Legasov's things lying on the table. It starts tapping. It is throbbing, like a child's heart.

Figure 2. Academician V. Legasov

* * *

"How clever are the Japanese people! They constructed a musical dosimeter. There is no cracking, just music, which sounds louder and louder."

Alexender A. Borovoi

A voice out of the corner: "It will be nice to have in the beginning Mendelssohn's Wedding March, which then goes fluidly into Chopin's Funeral March."

* * *

A hospital. My mother lies there barely moving, hardly speaking. During the day I work in the Institute, and then I come to her. There are not many nurses; they have time only to give injections and pills. There is nobody to give food to my mother, especially to persuade her to take every small piece of food, to swallow every spoonful of water. She knows I'm working in an operative group, helping Chernobyl with calculations and experiments, and suddenly she tells me:

"Sonny boy, do go there. I'll be better soon. You must go. I know this, I feel this. Chernobyl is your star. You can't leave your destiny, your place is there. Don't care about me. God blesses you!"

I went to Chernobyl the next day, after her funeral.

* * *

I can't keep all this in my heart.

2. Gravity of First Decisions

I'm going to write, based on my own memory, about the events that took place before my eyes and to describe my impressions about them. These notes are exclusively private things, and they don't aspire to give a detailed description of the Chernobyl tragedy.

I would like to avoid descriptions of those events that I didn't participate in. But sometimes it is impossible to understand our work without these details.

* * *

In the early morning of April 26, 1986, at 1:23 a.m., mistakes by the personnel working at Unit 4 of the Chernobyl Nuclear Power Plant, multiplied by mistakes of the RBMK reactor—the high power channel-type reactor—caused the most serious accident in atomic energy.

That April night has been described many times. I have seen a lot of books, booklets, and articles, and I am sure that this is not even half of everything written. I spoke to the witnesses, the workers at the plant, but that was some months after the accident, and their stories had the studied character of frequent repetitions.

I was interested in human reaction, human behavior in emergencies.

The general picture was the following.

In most cases, everyday workers displayed great courage

and responsibility after the accident. They realized that these events had dangerous consequences, but they didn't have enough information to estimate the real extent of the disaster.

Authorities at different levels tried to interpret the known information in the most soothing manner—and the higher the authority's level was, the more obvious this manner was. They weren't preventing the creation of panic—and they often talked about this later—so much as they were trying to distort the objective picture of those terrible events.

Although the majority of people demonstrated courage during the disaster, they weren't brave enough to tell the truth to others, or to come to serious decisions. Unit 3, situated in the same building with the unsafe Unit 4, went on working. Ventilation of Units 1 and 2 went on working also, gradually filling the rooms with radioactive aerosols. More and more people were affected by nuclear radiation.

The morning of April 26 came. In the daylight, the damages in Unit 4 became well-defined.

The roof of the building no longer existed. A part of the destroyed walls formed an obstruction on the northern side. The upper stories of the block, adjacent to the reactor's building, were also ruined. The roof of the Machine Hall, with its turbogenerators, was broken and burned in many places. On the ground near the Unit and on the roofs of the nearest buildings were graphite blocks and parts of uranium assemblies, thrown there by the explosion. It's difficult to describe this picture. A simple enumeration of the destruction took dozens of pages.

Figure 3. The generator building.

Alexender A. Borovoi

But the most serious anxiety was caused not by the signs of terrible damages, but by the column of smoke and steam rising out of the ruins. With this smoke, radioactivity spread into the atmosphere; and, as was discovered soon, it was measured by thousands, even tens of thousands, of Curies per hour.

That meant tens of thousands of square kilometers of contaminated territory, and hundreds of thousands of ruined futures for people.

* * *

In this catastrophic situation, on the evening of April 26, the Government Commission started its work. Everybody waited for immediate and effective decisions. According to the notions of that time, everybody expected wonders. But there are no wonders in techniques, and the quickness and effectiveness of any decision depended upon objective and subjective reasoning.

The first of those reasons was the extensive damage and the highest radiation fields inside and around Unit 4. The doses of radiation in these fields could be measured by the thousands of roentgen per hour. No one could go into the ruins of the reactor, the inner rooms, to learn the location and condition of the almost two hundred tons of nuclear fuel that had been in the reactor. High radioactivity had been kept inside the reactor of Unit 4 during the two and a half years of its working time.

There were many other reasons that didn't allow for decisions to be made quickly. Among them was the absence of necessary instruments and means of protection. One can write a separate book about the fact that the majority of existing technical means were absolutely useless in the conditions of an accident of this type.

But some subjective difficulties were met, especially during the crucial initial period. Among them were: already relayed information that minimized the extent of the accident; the expectation of immediate successes and vigorous reports for leaders; the statement that our reactors were absolutely safe, as had been propagandized for many years.

"Reactors do not explode," answered the minster who was responsible for the nuclear industry, when he was called up that night.

Hundreds of urgent questions required answers. It was necessary to select the most important problems among them and to formulate them correctly. As far as nuclear fuel was concerned, it presented three types of hazard at once:

- nuclear hazard
- thermal hazard
- radioactive hazard

Nuclear hazard: the beginning of a spontaneous, self-maintaining chain nuclear reaction (CNR). It could begin in the destroyed fuel, impregnated with water, but most likely between the safe remains of the reactor's assembly—if there were any after the explosion. The point is that a channel reactor of such high power is very big, and its separate parts can work independently.

How hazardous could the consequences of a CNR in the destroyed Unit have been?

During a long period of time, the hazard was exaggerated. It is being exaggerated today. In the beginning, this was due to a lack of confidence in the specialists' reports—and the Chernobyl accident didn't help to strengthen this confidence. Later, it was because of private interests and the influence of mass-media reports.

And then, in the first day after the accident, there were a number of efforts to measure the neutron streams around the Unit's ruins. Their great quantity was supposed to indicate that the reactor was continuing to work, uncontrollably.

Academician Legasov also tried to carry out such measuring near the reactor's ruins, risking his life.

* * *

Many months later, sitting in a small room stuffed with three tables, a stand, and a safe, Legasov unexpectedly told us about this episode. He told the story as an example of the human condition, when people realize for the first time the extent of an accident and the dimensions of the coming disaster.

"If I hadn't been in that condition," he said, "I would have understood at once that the instrument was useless. It wouldn't have worked in such high fields of gamma radiation, whether there were neutrons there or not. It would have choked. I understood it too late, when I was near the ruins. But we didn't have the necessary instruments. We had nothing to take with us."

"You didn't need to go, even with a good instrument," I said from my corner, surprising even myself. "Your trip was useless. Chain reactions in such conditions wouldn't last for even a minute. If masses of fuel formed and a CNR started, everything would get hot and fall to pieces."

Legasov, usually very patient and correct, especially in Chernobyl, stopped talking at once, controlling himself. We didn't have any more talks for three days.

He might have been right. I didn't understand the most important thing: during those first minutes, it was necessary to explode the atmosphere of passive despair, to start effective actions, to instill belief, even while risking one's life.

* * *

Thermal hazard: sometimes called the China Syndrome, also caused fear and anxiety. This name, taken from the 1979 film of the same name, means that nuclear fuel, which gets hot because of residual afterheat, starts to burn through the floors of a reactor's buildings one by one, going down until it reaches underground waters and contaminates them.

And last, radioactive hazard: it was there, growing every hour. With every release of smoke, radioactivity contaminated more and more territories.

Sleepless nights in Chernobyl, sleepless nights in Kiev, sleepless nights in Moscow.

What should we do?

3. Where Are the Thrown Materials?

On a videocassette, kept in closed archives for a few years and only recently made available for demonstrations, one can see a helicopter coming from the northeast toward the destroyed Unit. You hear the husky voice of a tired man: "On the stack! On the stack! Hundred meters up to the object. Fifty ... thirty... throw! Come on! Late!" And then there are some untranslatable Russian expressions.

The helicopter passes the stack, heading for Units 3 and 4, and at that moment it throws a load. The load falls down into the ruins, and the whole building shakes as if it had been bombed (fig. 3).

Figure 4. The helicopter flies up to Unit 4

This scene could be observed starting April 27 and for many days after. The best military pilots, transferred from Afghanistan, bombed the destroyed reactor with different materials. These materials were to fall into the reactor, where a whitish smoke spread, to form a barrier to nuclear, radioactive, and thermal hazards.

First, they threw materials containing boron. These were to prevent spontaneous chain reactions, because boron is one of the most effective neutron absorbers. Putting some dozens of kilograms of boron into a working reactor is enough to stop its nuclear reaction forever. But during the first days after the accident, they threw about forty tons of boron-containing materials into the reactor's ruins, thousands of times more than should have been needed. In this way, they fought against nuclear hazard.

Other materials were also thrown in. They were intended to fill the reactor's pit and form a filtering barrier to stop the spreading radioactivity. Among them were clay, sand, and dolomite. Two thousand six hundred tons during the first days.

Last, various things that contained metallic plumbum—lead—were thrown: shot, billets, and other items. The lead was supposed to melt when it came into contact with the hot materials of the reactor. In this way, it would neutralize some of the heat-release. To prevent China Syndrome, about 2400 tons of lead materials were thrown into the reactor.

According to the initial plan, the pit of the reactor was to be covered gradually with dry substances. That would diminish radioactive release, and at the same time reduce the heat. Experts considered that these combined actions would cause a decrease in the release, then an increase—a breaching—of hot gases, and then a final decrease.

Many reasons prevented these experts from correctly estimating the quantity of released activity. Mistakes in measuring were immense. Nevertheless, these measurements showed first the decrease of radioactive release, and then the increase. And then ... hurrah! The release was diminished by hundreds of times. It happened on the evening of May 6.

At Chernobyl, practice allowed for the perfect demonstration of the theory's calculations. And that fact was considered incontestable for three years. In many instances, it is the same today.

But by 1989-90, it became obvious that the majority of thrown materials didn't fall into the reactor's pit and didn't fulfill their tasks. The combination of rated and measured curves should, most likely, be considered a result of the "hypnotic influence" of high science upon the results of incorrect measuring.

Let's consider some facts.

The first one. Consider the Central Hall of the reactor. It's covered by huge hills of thrown materials. This could be observed from the helicopters before completion of the Shelter that encased the reactor; and it was proved by the exploratory groups that got inside the hall after a long preparatory period. But this doesn't exclude the fact that the major part of the materials landed in the reactor's pit.

The second fact. In the middle of 1988, with the help of optical instruments and TV cameras, researchers managed to see what was inside the pit of the reactor. They found practically no thrown materials. But here one can object that these materials fell into an area of extraordinarily high temperatures, and they melted and spread over the lower rooms of the reactor. Such a process could take place. On the lower floors, they did discover great accumulations of solid lava-like masses that contained nuclear fuel.

The third fact. The presence of lead would indicate that those lava-like masses contained not only materials of the reactor itself—concrete, dolomite, sand, steel, zirconium, etc.—but also materials thrown from the helicopters. But there is no lead in the reactor and the nearest rooms, even though over two thousand tons of it was thrown in! After investigation of dozens of samples, it was found that the quantity of lead in the lava masses was too small. That meant the lead didn't get into the pit. The other components of the thrown materials fell in such a small quantity, they couldn't influence the behavior of the release.

These are the known facts.

The location of the one-hundred-fifty-meter stack; the immense "upper cover" of the reactor, standing almost vertically; hundreds of other wrenched stacks—this geometry, formed as a result of the accident, prevented the successful throws of the various materials.

Does that mean everything was in vain?

That there was no point in the actions of military pilot Captain Sergey Volodin, who was the first to fly in the radioactive smoke right above the pit of the reactor to mark the terrible place?

Was it in vain when Colonel B. Nesterov threw the first bag with sand and marked the path of the flight?

No, one shouldn't think like that.

Boron-containing materials got into the Central Hall, where there were numerous fragments of active zone and fuel dust that had been thrown during the explosion. When they fell on the fuel, these materials made it nuclear safe.

Sand, clay, dolomite covered a thick layer of radioactive materials in many places, and later they made the work of constructors and researchers easier.

A small portion of these materials got into the pit and facilitated the forming of the lava.

What is more important: we needed about three years of really hard work to realize these facts.

* * *

And now on the same videotape, we see again a helicopter above the Unit. A husky voice gives commands, and the Unit collapses because of another falling load.

4. Teachers

I'm writing these lines on the 4th of February 1994. Anatoly Petrovich Alexandrov died today. Ex-Director of our Institute and ex-President of the Academy of Science of the ex-USSR. One of the main creators of atomic weapons, the atomic navy, and atomic plants. He was ninety years old. He had very little free time or vacation in his long life.

No one is treated equally by others, especially people of his stature. They may have a lot of well-wishers and admirers, but the number of their enemies is almost the same. I, without any doubt, rank myself among his admirers.

In 1968, I had the good fortune to have a long talk with him for the first time, when I was defending my candidate dissertation. Alexandrov was the head of the science committee, and we had different opinions on the subject of my dissertation. In my report, I spoke a lot about the necessity of my work, but Alexandrov, speaking after the positive reviews from official opponents, announced at once that nobody needed this particular premise in physics.

The piquancy of the situation was that, in fact, this premise was almost imposed upon our laboratory by Alexandrov's deputy, who was absent during my defense. This work was most likely forced upon me according to some pedagogical purposes. After a year of torture, I came to the decision, unexpectedly for everyone, to complete this task.

And now, listening to Alexandrov's speech, I realized that high above me, in the management office, there was a great war for and against the continuation of this premise, and

Alexender A. Borovoi

Alexandrov was against.

The situation was extremely bad.

I remember that the face of the head of our laboratory grew unusually light-green.

When this situation took place, the times did not allow one to speak in public against the Director, President, and Member of Party Central Committee. I had only one thing to do: to defend myself. This procedure is called "defense," and I had nothing to lose. So, in my last speech, I said with the courage of a doomed man that I had really fulfilled a difficult task; that the offered method was already being used as a solution for other problems of nuclear physics; and if the management had had doubts about the necessity of this premise, they should have thought everything over before, not after the fulfillment of this task.

Alexandrov listened and suddenly smiled.

The vote was unanimous—all voted "pro."

Alexandrov and I did not speak again for a long time.

* * *

I was working on the second floor of a three-story building called Central. Our institute began with this building. In 1943, when the building wasn't yet finished, I. V. Kurchatov and a few colleagues started working on atomic weapons. Later, on the third floor, offices for management were set up. They are still there.

The number of offices in the building was constantly increasing, and they practically superseded the laboratories on the first and second floors. After Kurchatov's death, Alexandrov, as manager, took his office. I greeted the manager

My Chernobyl

at our short daily meetings on the stairs; and for twenty years, our talks were restricted to these greetings.

On Friday, April 25, 1986, it was a sunny, cool day in Moscow. After the Institute's seminar, Alexandrov came back to Central by foot. Having watched for him, I joined him and started talking about the idea of a new installation that could register the neutron radiation of an atomic reactor. He was walking slowly, listening to me with interest—I thought—and asking questions. At last he invited me to his office on Tuesday, in four days, to make a detailed report with pictures and drawings.

He and I didn't know that at that moment in Pripyat, Ukraine, a modern and prestigious town of nuclear energy, not far from the ancient town of Chernobyl, buried in blooming fruit gardens, preparations for an experiment in Unit 4 of the Chernobyl Nuclear Power Plant had begun.

It was two o'clock of April 25, 1986.

At that moment, a female controller from Kiev called the Chernobyl Power Plant and demanded—!—the plant stop decreasing the power in the fourth reactor and postpone the tests. Eternal fear before any authorities, any order, worked. They postponed the tests, and the Unit continued working at decreased power for nine hours.

It was a dangerous regime.

Xenon poisoning—with which it's difficult to operate a reactor—started increasing. Let's avoid giving technical details and just say that this was the first step into the embrace of the accident.

After the Chernobyl accident, I spoke with Alexandrov often. About this and about his role in the accident, as I understand it, I will speak later. I will say that in the end of

Alexender A. Borovoi

May, I was sent with some papers to the Academy of Sciences, to Alexandrov's office. There were no people, no secretary in the waiting room. I opened the door and looked into the president's office. Alexandrov was sitting up straight and staring directly ahead. I realized by some elusive signs that he was not just in deep thought, but was in despair. I couldn't come in.

He was eighty-three years old, and around the same time as the Chernobyl accident, his wife died. I think the spring of 1986 divided his life into two halves—a triumphal half and a hopeless one. The last one took almost eight years.

He was berated with endless accusations, often rough and unprofessional. But he behaved with high dignity, went on working, and helped us in Chernobyl as he could (fig. 5).

Figure 5. The Academician A. Alexandrov (in the center) on Unit 4

My Chernobyl

* * *

My mother was right. Life gradually and quietly prepared me for Chernobyl, probably as early as school.

Having learned that I was going to be a physicist—and not a plain physicist, but an atomic one—my school teachers gave me some additional lessons. Without any payment, of course. I applied for the Moscow Engineering Physical University in a difficult competition. Six people, all graduating from school with medals, competing for one place. I chose this university not only for my future profession as a specialist in nuclear physics—I had a vague idea about this—but also for its prestige and because girls who were my close friends liked the words *secret* and *radioactivity*.

Later, everything was quite successful.

First—I had very good teachers. Clever scientists and interesting people. Belyaev, Budker, Gurevich taught me. I attended lectures of Nobel Prize winners—Cherenkov and Landau. The latter was God in our minds. He even looked like a biblical prophet. After the lectures, we, a quiet and excited crowd, followed our idol. Sometimes he noticed us and entered into our talks, or asked his favorite questions. Once, Landau asked us to give a definition for happiness.

How could a physicist define this word? Nobody among the students had thought over this question before. The sensation of happiness for a twenty-year-old man didn't demand any deep philosophical ground.

Landau said, "Happiness—when you give yourself a difficult but a solvable task." Then he gave an explanation for those who didn't understand. "If the task is easy, you can't feel any pleasure in solving it. If the problem is too difficult to solve,

Alexender A. Borovoi

and you can't come to any decision, you may get an inferiority complex."

Everybody was delighted. Imagine, a great scientist spoke to us and made such extraordinary statements. What can I say after such a course of time? I am not a great philosopher, but I think that decisions for difficult tasks are not always enough for happiness. Happiness is an individual thing; and now I am happy when I know that somebody is waiting for me, that my dearly loved people need me.

* * *

When I came to the Kurchatov Institute, I met Peter Spivak as my teacher. He was a good experimenter, a kind and decent person, but he liked to look severe and start arguments. More than that, he was very lively. Catching me out in mistakes and in ignorance, he would berate me and at the same time jump up and down on one leg. When his accusations grew harsher, the height of his jumps rose until they were about one foot. At that moment, his left hand would turn to the ceiling, maybe to the sky, and his right hand was directed on me, showing that I was some distance from the high ideals of physics.

He demanded steady fulfillment of many rules, almost laws, of experimental physics. To write down everything and to do it properly, even those things that seem unimportant. To finish each test with the measurement you started with, to be sure that nothing changed and nothing was broken, etc. And the main thing: to think over every detail and calculate everything beforehand. Don't be in a panic when you get into radioactive fields.

Once, I was impertinent enough to ask him who his

teachers were. Spivak explained to me for a very long time that I should know the history of physics, and then he told me with pride: "My teacher was Ioffe!" Without any thought, I asked, "Who was Ioffe's teacher?" My leader didn't start jumping, he just growled, "Röntgen, the famous Röntgen!"

"Then why are you so excited, Peter Efimovich?" I babbled. Just think, please, that this chain stopped existing with me.

If I could only know how often we mentioned the name of the great Röntgen, sometimes without any need. Even in my dreams I see those dark rooms and hear the voice of a dosimetrist shouting, "One roentgen. Five, be careful! Forty roentgen! We can't go farther!" In the destroyed Unit nobody, of course, could say the whole phrase, "The dose is one hundred roentgen per hour!" Nobody had time for that.

* * *

Second—for those who haven't forgotten what was the first—I had very good pupils. My friends and I organized an evening school where the pupils of senior classes studied—those who had extraordinary abilities in physics and mathematics, or those who thought they had great gifts for them. My dear pupils, the majority of whom became candidates or doctors of science, started in their turn to teach me physics using methods that were difficult for me. They observed with great pleasure my convulsions at the blackboard as I tried to solve them. At last I was able to orientate quickly, and got good enough with the questions of general physics. It helped me a lot later. Especially in the dark ruins of Unit 4, when I had reached an urgent decision, having nothing with me but plastic clothes, a torch, and a dosimeter.

Alexender A. Borovoi

So, I worked in the Kurchatov Institute, the leader of one small group of colleagues. And then Chernobyl happened.

5. My Mother

I was introduced to my mother when I was twenty-seven years old. During the Great Patriotic War of 1941–1945, she divorced my father and left for some distant place. I was three years old then, and my mother left not recollections but some sensations for me—sensations of her affection and the wonderful smell of her hair. Our lives took such a turn that we started to meet when I was grown up, with a fully formed personality. My wife and I went to see her, and our visits became more frequent because her house was extremely interesting. The people you could meet at her evening teas! Art critics—Mother's husband was one of the most famous specialists in India art; priests—my mother was very religious; successful and not so successful writers; famous doctors and people who posed as doctors; famous conjurers and telepaths seeking audiences and glory. This varied company was united by only one thing—my mother's charm. When I write the word *charm*, it expresses only to a small extent the great appeal of this elderly but still very attractive woman (fig. 6).

* * *

Sometimes even I, a proponent of exact sciences and a person far removed from mysticism and religion, thought that my mother was a sorceress.

You can judge it for yourself. Using cards, my mother often told women's fortunes. For a long time, I paid no attention to their excited opinions about the results of this fortune-telling,

Alexender A. Borovoi

relegating them to the sphere of self-hypnosis and my mother's worldly insights. One evening, a young lady came with a friend of my mother's to see her. This lady was greatly interested in her future for reasons she didn't mention. After much persuasion, Mother agreed to look at the cards. I was sitting quietly in the corner of the next room, reading. They didn't notice me.

Figure 6. My mother, twenty years old

Mother looked at this lady intently. "Your name is Lida, isn't it?"

"Yes, I told you this when we met."

"You are married and your husband's name is Volodya."

"Yes, but how do you know this?" Lida turned to their mutual friend. "Did you tell this ?"

"No, I told her nothing."

"And," my mother said, "you want to know something about a woman named Maria. You think that your husband is in love with her."

There was undisguised horror in Lida's voice. "How do you know everything? Nobody in the whole world heard about this!"

I won't describe the rest of their conversation, but later I asked my mother how she could guess names during her fortune-telling. She answered that she didn't know. When she got into the necessary mood—and sometimes she failed to— the names just flashed in her mind. And not only the people's names, but also names of towns, numerals, and dates of some events. I felt that she told me the truth. She was too proud a person to play tricks or to lie. My scientific view didn't change, but I had a feeling similar to a fear of dark rooms. Some years later, absolutely accidentally, I found an explanation to this apparent mindreading.

It happened in Ural, in a small town, or even a village, called Sim. There, I. V. Kurchatov was born. Maintaining a tradition, the most talented senior pupils from the whole Ural gathered there every summer to listen to lectures. I gave a lecture in physics, and in the next room there were some lessons in either psychology or psychiatry. I had no interest at first. But later, pupils started to talk about the extraordinary things they learned there. The lecturer was a woman, a professor from one of the secret institutes, and she demonstrated things that seemed wondrous but had easy explanations. I was very curious about this, and after a short debate with the organizers, the physics lectures were held earlier and I was able to attend the woman's lecture. It was extremely interesting. She needed volunteers for her experiments, and with the youngest people afraid of looking funny, I participated in all the experiments. After the lecture, using the rights of an experimental rabbit, I told her the story about my mother's fortune-telling and asked for explanations. The professor explained everything to me, calling this phenomenon *Gypsy effect*.

"I saw this at Gypsy's places," she said. "To guess the names, fortune-tellers should possess a gift for hypnosis. When she looks very hard at a client and says, 'Your name ...', there is a pause, and the client's lips start moving automatically and pronounce their name. The most interesting thing here is that neither the client nor the fortune-teller suspect this mechanism. Reading the client's lips passes her consciousness, and this thing seems for one person a wonder of guessing, and for the other person a wonder of illumination."

So, not up to the end, but to some extent, one of my mother's secret was revealed.

* * *

My mother fell ill frequently, and as I recall went to hospitals several times. When the doctors' rounds were over, there was a crowd of women near her bed, asking her for fortune-telling and just talking.

My Chernobyl

In the beginning of 1986, she was in a hospital again. We soon realized she would never sit at her dining table again and listen attentively and with sympathy to a new request for fortune-telling.

It was April.

* * *

Chernobyl started for me the evening of April 29.

The manager of our department, Academician S. Belyaev, called me up and asked me, very politely, whether I could come and help with calculations for Chernobyl. Of course, I agreed. On the way there, it occurred to me that it was strange that in a department where there are many bright theorists, an experimental physicist had been called. Later, I understood that the majority of theorists were not acquainted with nuclear energy at all, and that there were some theorists who disagreed with it according to some "principal reasons." "They didn't foresee the accident," was the response, "so let them solve the problem for themselves." Who "they" were wasn't defined. These comments could be heard from other specialists. It was an elementary fear: Suppose they would be sent to Chernobyl? It was better to have no attitude about it.

The evening passed into night, and my long odyssey began.

* * *

A hospital. My mother lies there barely moving, hardly speaking. During the day I work in the Institute, and then I come to her. There are not many nurses; they have time only to give injections and pills. There is nobody to give food to my mother, especially to persuade her to take every small piece of food, to swallow every spoonful of water. She knows I'm working in an operative group, helping Chernobyl with calculations and experiments.

When I said the word *Chernobyl* to my mother for the first time, she remembered that chernobyl is a sort of wormwood, a bitter steppe grass. And suddenly she says to me, "Take a Bible and find The Revelation of St. John the Divine."

I open the Bible and see at once words so often repeated in articles and books.

> And the third angel sounded, and there fell a great star from heaven, burning as it were a lamp, and it fell upon the third part of the rivers, and upon the fountains of waters; And the name of the star is called Wormwood: and the third part of the waters became wormwood; and many men died of waters, because they were made bitter. 8:10-11 (King James)

My mother looks at me intently. "Sonny boy, do go there. I'll be better soon. You must go. I know this, I feel this. Chernobyl is your star. You can't leave your destiny, your place is there. Don't care about me. God blesses you!"

I went to Chernobyl the next day, after her funeral.

Chernobyl — 1986

1. First Steps

Memory is a wonderful thing. It lets me down often, especially when I try to reproduce some event of my school years, or some of my work in the Institute. And I have to base some memories on special dates, to enumerate those events chronologically, sometimes using a pencil to write them down. But I can easily reproduce almost every day, even every minute, of my long-lasting Chernobyl epic, especially the years of 1986–88.

So, Chernobyl of 1986.

* * *

A town without inhabitants. The major parts of buildings are boarded up, but one can walk past houses where everything is still open, and see things left all over the place. The owners might have left the houses in a hurry, or somebody might intend to live there again, or this might be the consequences of looting.

In the streets there are people in special dark coveralls, which look like prisoner uniforms, many of them with white masks on. Respirators. Military technicians. Watering machines pass constantly, pressing the dust with waterjets.

Suddenly I see an old woman carrying a sack. She wears a usual jacket, a skirt, and has no mask. I help her to hoist the sack into a truck. It opens, and some ragged beggar things fall out. The woman kisses me and makes the sign of a cross over me (fig. 7).

Figure 7. An abandoned house in Chernobyl.

Gardens are full of fruit trees. A lonely hen searches for a refuge. Do they really shoot domestic animals?

Constant anxiety can be seen in how people move and in their faces.

* * *

Pripyat, a wide and a beautiful river. There are some ships on it, near the island. They are still there, decrepit and rusty. One can dip into the water, but should avoid walking along the bank of the Pripyat.

When radioactivity falls onto the surface of water, it subsides quickly and is seized by the aquatic plants at the bottom. They cling to the smallest particles of nuclear fuel that were expelled with the explosion. This can be perfectly seen from a helicopter during measurements. When a helicopter passes the territory of the power plant, all instruments show high contamination. Hardly is the helicopter above the water when all indicators decrease by hundreds of times. Radiation from the plant is absorbed by the water, but the water itself is comparatively clear.

As for the banks, though, where there is silt and river dust cast up by waves, they are highly contaminated by radioactivity.

* * *

The church. The doors are locked, and there is no opportunity even to come close to it. There is barbed wire around it, and where the wire ends, there is a barrier and posted sentries. Around the church—accidentally? purposefully?—a military unit is situated. There are armfuls of fresh flowers on the church's porch. Every time I came to this place during those long Chernobyl days of the '86 year, there always were flowers. And always absolutely fresh.

* * *

The Government Commission was situated in a two-story house on the square. Facing the house, where the City Committee worked earlier, the Lenin monument stood. Later, when we happened to work in this building for many hours in a row, and our heads refused to think at all, we usually walked up to this monument and back. We called this walking "To go and consult Ilyich."

Alexender A. Borovoi

* * *

The operative group of the Kurchatov Institute is situated on the ground floor. As I enter, I am very surprised. What a trifling-sized building with such a famous and long name! The leader of the operative group starts complaining to me at once.

"Why have you and not such-and-such person come? Where is the discipline?"

I realize he is awfully tired, and I try to relieve the tension.

"You are speaking to me like a professor whose lectures only two people came to listen to. He is shouting and reproaching them, and neglecting the subject. But they are the people who came, and they should be praised, not cursed."

He laughs and orders me to go to the first floor and introduce myself to somebody in the Government Commission, because now I am a kind of consultant. On the first floor, the next lesson is waiting for me. I walk into the room and address an elderly and respectable-looking man. He doesn't listen to me, just shouts: "Can you speak in Russian? Who are you?"

I answer, saying my name, my institute, but he does not soften. "Can you name your profession?"

"Yes, I can. I am a physicist."

"We don't need physicists here. For what damned reason are physicists here? We need specialists for reactors!"

"Specialists for reactors did everything they could for you already."

He looks at me with widely opened eyes and shows me to the door. It is quite obvious my new chief doesn't like me at all.

* * *

I spent the whole day on my feet. I was running around Kiev, then around Chernobyl, ate nothing, and had no ideas where to sleep. Only in the evening did I manage to get into the hostel where Kurchatovers lived. I knew many of them quite well. None of them was interested in my job; everybody was just happy to have additional working arms. I was led to the canteen and then offered to take the bed of a fellow who worked in the night shift. There were not enough beds for us all.

2. Some Words About My Work and Everyday Life

Faces of my colleagues who worked during this time in the operative group of the Kurchatov Institute are again before my eyes. There were about twenty to thirty of them. The number was constantly changing. Usually a small group came to Chernobyl, having prepared its equipment in Moscow, and worked there for a few days, or weeks, or months. If the term was longer, the staff periodically changed. Some people were in Chernobyl once and never came back. Others returned to the Zone again after a short rest in Moscow. For many of them, the Chernobyl epic lasted for months and years. As I write, I am coming to my tenth year.

Our work there was extremely interesting and absorbing. The members of the operative group were constantly aware of the necessity and significance of their work, and that feeling is a great stimulus for any person. And the condition of happiness, formulated some time ago by Landau, was fulfilled. We settled and settled quite successfully everything that was beyond our power, any difficult task.

There existed one more circumstance. After the accident, specialists managed, although not for a long time, to make the frightened official and managerial authorities help us.

During the years of my work in the Institute, I realized and resigned myself to the thought that any half-educated supply agent, any girl from the accounts department or from the Secretariat, could give any command to a scientist without any obstacle. These people, intentionally or accidentally, blackmailed the specialists with their ability to interfere with the work they did.

In the Chernobyl of 1986, the wave of general sympathy for the workers in the Zone, the strict and often vehement position of the Government Commission—everything made various services work. Everybody tried to help, if only so they could look like they were helping.

Even such a concentration of underground power, like trade, was fought sometimes. Effectively or not? That is another question.

* * *

I remember, at one session of the Government Commission, seeing two ordinary civilian suits and an elegant lady's raincoat among the plain working clothes. They were two men and a woman—trade authorities—who made a report. They presented posters with colored diagrams and graphs. These graphs displayed increase of places for trade and sale. Increases of all possible achievements. Their quiet audience listened to the list of goods arriving to Chernobyl from all countries of the world. The goods were sold in the shops situated outside the Zone where the workers lived—or, to be more exact, had time to sleep for a few hours. As far as Kurchatovers were concerned, we lived in Chernobyl, worked at the station, and never heard about caviar, coffee, Austrian shoes, French cosmetics, and Canadian leather coats in our shops. The first time we learned about all of these goods was at this session. As it turned out later, we were not alone in this.

One of the trade authorities was speaking fluently and confidently, and I turned my eyes from the graphs to the

Alexender A. Borovoi

Chairman. By this time—it was autumn of 1986—I had begun to understand him, and I saw some definite signs that this report couldn't end with only applause.

"Have you finished?" the Chairman finally asked politely. He always needed some kind of an initial run. "Very good. So, during the previous three days, all the shoes were sold to Chernobyl workers, weren't they?"

"Yes, they were, Mr. Chairman."

"And nothing is left in the shops and the warehouses?"

"Yes. Practically nothing is left. Our duty is to give everything to our heroes of Chernobyl."

The Chairman kept his silence for a while.

"You see, it's very strange," he said, addressing the audience. "In the morning, all members of the Government Commission were divided into groups and visited all the shops that were to sell the shoes. We asked hundreds of people. Nobody saw or heard about foreign shoes. I suppose that all shoes were sold by some underground way and in some other places. These are the results of your work, but not this lie we have been listening to for a whole hour! Are there any representatives of the Prosecutor's Department here?"

I should mention that at every session of the Government Commission, there were the highest ranks from the Union and the Ukrainian Prosecutor's Departments. These people stood up.

"It is necessary to initiate proceedings against this prospering gang immediately," the Chairman said. "And the report they presented today should be considered as material for investigation. It is only suitable in this case."

The trade authorities looked awfully bad.

My Chernobyl

* * *

We were all deeply impressed by this case; and then rumors about it, flavored with various inventions and fantasies, were spread around the Zone, and even widely outside it. I suspect that was the aim of this act. The Government Commission displayed high principles, and then continued to work on the long list of technical-engineering questions. The Zone in this period presented a combination of wonderful, honest, and sometimes heroic work with almost unconcealed and impudent idleness and stealing. Proportions of the first and the second changed over time, and, unfortunately, not for the best.

* * *

So, if in 1986, the structures that hindered our work were neutralized somehow, the situation quickly became quite the same. And the reconstruction of our society—perestroika— just made it worse.

* * *

And now I would like to describe in a few words our everyday Chernobyl life. Our hostel, which was also a laboratory, was in the building of the gynecological department of the Chernobyl municipal hospital. At first sight, this choice seemed strange, but it can be understood if you take into consideration that it was very easy to decontaminate the rooms of the gynecology. The majority of them were tiled, the walls and ceilings were covered with white oil paint, and the tables and other furniture were made of stainless steel. There were two shower rooms and a bathroom. Almost ideal conditions for decontamination.

For many years, the building was still called gynecology, becoming "laboratory" later. An occasional witness would be shocked if he heard talk between two gloomy and unshaven men, when one said to the other: "Your place is in the gynecology. It was a hard job to get, and you are wandering in the streets. You should go there immediately."

By the time I arrived, the initial radioactive cleanliness, or just cleanliness, had gotten lost. A part of the room was used for sleeping; another part, for work. In the latter, workers counted, drew, prepared instruments, and graduated them with the help of radioactive sources. Instruments in need of repair were also brought into those rooms. They were brought after work at the station and after decontamination, which might be done without care. Or not done at all. Tired people, almost always after sleepless nights, forgot to take off their coveralls. If they did take them off, they threw them anywhere. Of course, the division between bedrooms and working rooms was symbolic to an extent. They worked everywhere, where they managed to find a free corner. And made a mess everywhere.

As far as our hygiene was concerned, there was only one working shower for more than twenty people, and I don't want to remember the toilets.

One case helped us a lot. An engineer came from Moscow and took an instrument with him for work at the Unit. But this instrument wasn't completed. This man was very responsible and, almost living at his work table, he labored on the instrument for several days. When I would leave gynecology early in the morning and come back late at night, I always saw him at the table, soldering or screwing something.

At this time, our personal dosimeters—accumulators that registered doses of contamination a person got during his working time—were checked. Usually, these small badges were fastened to the outer part of our clothes, on our chests. Periodically, the dosimeters were examined in the laboratory, where they were "burned" in a special way, doses were measured, and then the badges were returned to their owners. With this procedure, the dosimeter "forgot" its previous history and was ready to register doses again.

We fought against dosimeters constantly and secretly.

The point was that a person having received a dose of 25 roentgen (25 R/h) should, according to the medical terms, leave Chernobyl immediately. With this, he got five months' salary. Good money in this time. Why 25 R/h was the limit, it is difficult for me to say. I am not a specialist. I just remembered for myself that if you got more than 100 R/h, you got radiation sickness.

When the authorities came to this decision, those working at the station became diametrically opposed to it. One pole—not very numerous—consisted of those who wanted to leave the Zone as soon as possible and with the five-month salary. These people, who aspired later to the reputation of Chernobyl heroes, usually tried to "forget" their accumulators and other types of dosimeters in dangerous, high-radiation places, and then would return secretly to get them. During the checking, the desired dose of 25 R/h was discovered; and if everything was done well and there was no evidence of swindle, the "hero" went back to his motherland with money and respect. There he started his struggle for privileges with more energy than a person who had actually gotten such a high dose could possibly have.

The major part of the Kurchatovers—and it did them credit—took the opposite pole. People who did research in areas with doses of hundreds and thousands roentgen per hour tried to leave their dosimeters in safe places, or to shield the instruments so that they couldn't register that fatal 25 R/h. Then they could stay in Chernobyl. This was the secret war with our accumulators. The authorities knew everything about it, but did nothing. They needed specialists like air.

One day there was a check in the laboratory, and they took all the workers' badges. After the measuring, everybody was absolutely bewildered. Those who worked at the Unit were examples of "good behavior," with readings of 10, 12, 15 R/h. And a person who constructed an instrument in the laboratory? This person had 30 R/h. How? Why?

Investigation showed that there was a mitten near him, on the next table. Somebody brought a small souvenir in it—a source that radiated about 1 R/h at a distance of 0.5 m—and it was right beside the engineer's work table. Considering this, it was easy to see that this person worked hard, because he spent thirty hours at the table over the course of only three days.

Nobody could laugh. Our colleague had "burned down"—our slang for receiving a high dose of radiation—and when burned down, a worker became absolutely useless. The owner of the mitten wanted to stay unknown, and the engineer with his instrument and five-month salary was sent home, and a Commission was sent from Moscow instead.

Thanks to this accident, two weeks after my arrival our everyday life was radically changed. Bath, showers, and everything else began working. Rooms were decontaminated, a medical post was organized, and so on. Of course, we didn't get absolute cleanliness, but how could we do that in the Chernobyl of 1986?

* * *

Our food was very good. And though the rooms of our canteens looked like prisons, because they were always dark, crowded with people in work clothes and hats—everything was in dark, dirty colors—the best Moscow restaurants could envy our food.

At the time of lunch or dinner, some abandoned animals—dogs, cats, hens—gathered at our canteen. Only after they had left, a fox came to the building very cautiously. Everybody loved it and defended it from the dogs. Its walk seemed strange to me: short and timid steps, always turning its head. Only later I learned that the fox was totally blind.

3. Shelter

The work of the operative group became more concentrated on the construction of the cover that was to encase the destroyed Unit 4. It was called "Shelter of the Fourth Unit," but later—by the light hand of a writer—it got a new name: Sarcophagus.

We have spoken already that on the sixth of May, ten days after the accident, the release of radioactivity out of the destroyed Unit, which threatened to cause serious disasters, decreased suddenly by hundreds of times. At the time, the reason for this decrease was considered to be the effect of all the materials that had been thrown from the helicopters. Now we know that those materials hadn't played their proper role. The explanation is different now. At that time, the fuel, having melted the lower protective plate of the reactor, dissolved in other melted materials and formed radioactive lava, never seen in nature before. Lava spread in the lower stores of the block and started to cool. The radioactive release was practically stopped.

China Syndrome—the burning of concrete plates and the gradual falling of the fuel— worked only for that lower plate and, to some extent, for the floor of the room situated right under the reactor.

Again, we only know this now. Then, in May of 1986, only one thing was absolutely clear: the situation was stabilizing somehow.

It was necessary to cover the open radioactive wound—the reactor's ruins—as soon as possible, to isolate it from the environment. Without this, a strong wind could spread dust out of it. Rain water could get into it, absorb radioactivity, and contaminate ground waters. And last, penetrating radioactivity threatened everybody working at the Station.

About eighteen various projects of Shelter were presented. To avoid the details, the projects can be divided into two groups. The first group consists of big constructions, covering with a hermetic cupola or hangar the whole building of Unit 4. The remaining buildings with radioactive materials would be kept inside Shelter. Thus, all destroyed buildings would be stored in the huge Shelter. The second group consists of projects that suggested using the remaining walls of Unit 4 as supports for new designs. That would greatly reduce the size of Shelter.

The second group was chosen. It ensured high benefits in time and cost of building.

I think the choice in that trying situation was absolutely right. Though, as it frequently happens, nobody thought about defects in the second group. Nobody tried to eradicate them. Those defects were not even mentioned.

What were the defects?

To use the existing constructions that remained after the explosion and fire, partially destroyed as they were, as supports for new constructions, it was necessary to be sure of their strength and stability, which required taking measurements. That was impossible to do. High radiation fields around and inside the Unit created obstacles. The majority of measurements had to be done from a helicopter, as a guess. That is why the real extent of the strength of the new constructions was practically unknown.

To work on the building right at the block and not at a

distance—as would have been done with the projects in the first group—it was possible only with the use of remote-controlled mechanisms. These mechanical devises were bought abroad quickly, unusual for our organizations. They were a number of special concrete pumps—Putzmeisters—which transported mortar through long hoses, controlled at a distance; and a number of cranes of high-carrying capacity—Demagy. These mechanisms ensured quick distance building. But ... At this building, it was impossible to use welding to form the constructions properly. And there remained numerous cracks in the original construction. Because of that, Shelter was not hermetic. Through these cracks, water and snow could get in, and radioactive dust could easily get out.

So, two main defects—that this construction wasn't hermetic and had indefinite strength—became the price for low cost and speed.

But we have run ahead.

Shelter doesn't exist yet. It is being built now with impressive speed (fig. 8).[2]

And I must find my place in Chernobyl yet.

---

[2] Construction of Shelter continued for 206 days and nights, from June to November 1986.

Figure 8. Putzmeister placing concrete in the "Shelter".

4. The Precepts

Night has passed, and my first working morning has come. I am going to the headquarters, and on my way I am thinking about my plans for the day. I was sent here as a physicist-consultant, but am I able to take on this job? Will they really need me?

All wait for the arrival of Academician Legasov. He is supposed to come by the middle of the day, but he doesn't appear until the evening, and starts listening to the reports and giving tasks. My turn is last.

"There is a problem to be solved as soon as possible," I begin. "On the ground from the west side of the block, a high dose was discovered. Too high to allow the people to work there—20-30 R/h. The source is unknown. It may be a wall of the block where it 'shines' through its windows and cracks. It may be the soil. The soil was covered with crushed stones and sand not a long time ago, but maybe this is not enough? You should discover the main source and choose the means of protection. What is your suggestion? You should do everything by tomorrow. The workers should start the day after tomorrow."

Everybody is facing me, silent, waiting. There is sympathy in their eyes—the authorities are checking up a new worker.

"We have to do everything on the place," I continue. "To take dosimeters, lead sheets. First of all, to measure with a dosimeter the dose in the place where people will be working, then to protect it against straight radiation with the sheets of lead. The so-called shady protection. If the dose decreases, it is clear. Mainly, the block shines. In that case, we can protect people with walls and screens. If everything remains the same, it means that radiation is everywhere. Soil shines. Then we should add some sand. This we could do if we were lucky. According to the law of maximum meanness, the first thing and the second thing are both shining. And we'll have to add sand and build wall obstacles. Yes, and we should take samples of soil in vertical tubes. To know how much sand is there and what quantity we should add."

"All right, do it," the Chairman says.

People relax, and many of them offer me their help. But I have got a good assistant already, an old colleague who also arrived yesterday. Besides, he is a very good driver, and we can't do without a car. We decide to go to Unit 4 early the next morning.

* * *

It is evening. I am sitting on my bed calculating the necessary thickness of lead. Without any hurry, two old residents from the Institute, already famous to me, come into the room. They are to go to Moscow tomorrow after their month shift, and I thought at first that they came just to say good-bye. But the point is not the farewell. They sit on the next bed—there is a lack of chairs in gynecology—and one says to me, "Al, listen carefully. To visit the block is not an easy task. You can't be there for a long time with only the knowledge you got in books and at the Institute. You shouldn't follow all the usual instructions on safety. If you do, you'd better stay at home, because in this case, you can do nothing. Everything is strictly forbidden. But as for the accident ... If you want to live and work here, you must know the rules of this game. Many people burned out here before they learned these rules. But if somebody else has learned them, there is no sense in acquiring your own experience. That is why you are to listen and to remember, as a grace."

The other fellow interrupts the talk. "They should not be called rules. *Precepts* sounds much better."

"Well, what should we call the first one? To sound better?"

"What? Ozone smell!"

* * *

"Why did so many people suffer right after this accident? Died, fell seriously ill, will fall ill and become invalids? Because they didn't even imagine what crazy fields of radiation stormed at the destroyed block and in the rooms of the reactor. And they went on working in their places in these high radiation fields. Sometimes it was really necessary, but I suppose it was often useless. They didn't realize the real situation because they didn't have the necessary instruments. There were some instruments that displayed no more than 3.6 R/h. And there were the fields with hundreds and thousands of R/h. There were some rumors that one person from the civil defense had a special instrument that displayed up to 200 R/h. But the authorities didn't want to believe this. And they didn't believe the other person whose instrument displayed 1000 R/h. They even tried to lose the graph he had made. They told us this at the Station.

"Now, about our plans. Tomorrow you are to take DP-5. It is a military instrument constructed for civil defense. It is very good for measurements when radiation behaves evenly and when the dose is not more than 200 R/h. But if the dose is near 2000? The pointer of this instrument moves very slowly, and you are standing there and your dose is increasing. And the last point on this—DP-5 is 200 R/h. What should you do?"

"How can I get out of this situation?" I asked.

"By using your own senses!"

"But a man doesn't feel radiation. Even in our books and in lectures, they say radiation has no color, no smell, no taste."

"This is only in lectures. The lecturers have been staying in Moscow and can't reach Chernobyl. High radiation fields have their smell. And if you smell this, don't display any heroism, but quickly—quickly—reel your fishing lines in and run away as fast as you can."

"What is the smell?"

"Ozone. The first precept: be afraid of the smell of ozone."

* * *

"The second percept is more plain: don't forget about the light. Suppose you are given the task to work at the block in already developed rooms. The lighting is very good, the lamps are bright. Do always take a torch with you everywhere. And matches also. Whether you smoke or you don't, you should always have matches with you. Do you need explanation? When the workers chop the power cable and leave all the rooms without lighting, you'll understand everything yourself."

* * *

"Water at the block is an unpleasant thing in general. But

water under your feet is something you are ready for. Plastic top-boots protect you against this kind of water. Of course, you shouldn't fall down. This precept is not about falling down. Be afraid of water falling from above! Care about the falling water. Entering any room, avoid the places where this could take place. It is very difficult to protect your face against the falling water. It could fall on your mask and then reach your eyes. There is no place at the block to wash faces and eyes properly. Do care about your eyes."

* * *

Our talk took a long time. They really had many percepts. I am very grateful to my friends for this talk, for their warnings, which helped me to avoid many "extra" roentgen. The members of the operative group passed these famous oral percepts on like a baton. But then, when the situation at the block was stabilizing, this tradition was forgotten.

* * *

Three times I got into extremely bad situations inside Shelter just because I violated those percepts. I will describe only the last case.

* * *

If there exists absolute darkness, this darkness is around me. The main thing: don't move. Because at this moment my visual memory keeps recollections about the room, the place where I am now. If I start moving, I will lose orientation at once. So, don't move, don't panic, do think everything over.

Electricity has been switched off for some minutes already, maybe for a half an hour. If electricians begin repairing the damages right now, then this won't be so terrible. I can stand several minutes in the darkness. But it is evening now. The work at the Unit is finished. In a night shift, only a few people are on duty. And they, of course, will put off repair work.

I can't wait for many hours. And not because of the external dose—it is not high—but because of the high concentration of plutonium dust in the air. Here my respirator, having worked for many hours and now moist, can't save me. It is good for some minutes—to look into a room and to go farther. But lepestok weren't constructed to serve an entire night.

I have neither a torch nor matches. I violated one of the percepts, and plutonium dust—we have fought against it constantly in recent years—has captured me in a very mean way.

The way back is difficult even at full lighting. I need to go downstairs by two fire ladders, pass through narrow passages—bending down—and make my way through scattered debris. It is possible, too, to get into the places where external radiation exists.

Will they try to find me? They will hardly do it. Officially, our working day was over, and my daily permission to work was closed out. Using the "privileges" of an old resident and a member of the authorities, I took the keys and decided to look into this room. I told my team, "I am coming soon. Go on without me." They'll wait in the bus for a while and then decide that I left by a "personal" car. But I sent my driver to Chernobyl. Nobody knows that.

The main thing is not to lose my mind and not to be in a

Alexender A. Borovoi

hurry to just go somewhere. Let's stand calmly and think. I have some time yet.

* * *

It was the fourth year after the accident—1990. With great difficulties, the rooms of the Unit were won back from radioactivity. They were won through bore-hammering devices and then setting lead detectors in the places of nuclear-fuel concentrations. The room where I was captured by darkness was settled a long time ago, more than a month. A hole was bored out of this room, and detectors were being prepared for installation.

The next hole was being bored near the first one, but then an emergency happened. Because of careless handling of the sample taken out of the hole, plutonium dust got into the room. At the last moment, the dosimetrists reported a sharp increase of plutonium concentration in the air, by several thousand times. Work was immediately stopped, the room was locked, and then I decided to look into it to see the situation...

* * *

What is there around me? What could help me? There is an assembly table here, with some parts of detectors, prepared for assembly, on it. If I am not mistaken, there is a coverall left by somebody. Why is there a coverall? Well, it is not important. The only thing that is important is that any coverall has pockets, and there may be matches and a respirator in them. If the person is so untidy to leave his coverall here, he may stealthily smoke here, at the block. Unfortunately, there are many similar examples of this happening here. Earlier this room was quite normal; radiation dose was very small, according to our standards. Nobody would want to go to the medical post to smoke. One could waste a lot of time and power walking back and forth. Well, I have persuaded myself. I have only to persuade in my mind the owner of this coverall: first, to smoke; second, to smoke at the Unit; and third, to leave matches in the pockets. Even if there are no matches, I have to come to the table, because a table is an object and not a dark vacuum.

But the room is very large, about fifty square meters. Maybe it seems large because I am now frightened? I should go toward the wall and then along the wall counterclockwise. Don't be in a hurry, you still have time.

The table, the coverall. There are pockets, but there are neither a respirator nor matches in them. What a brute! A man who doesn't smoke! But I don't smoke either. I don't smoke, but I don't leave coveralls and I don't break human hopes either! Let's think further. I have time.

Can it possibly be that I have nothing that shines, maybe even a little? No, it can't be! In my coveralls, in the upper pocket, I put my wristwatch with its shining dial. I am taking the watch out. The time is displayed perfectly well. I've spent a lot of time here already, more than an hour since I parted with the others. But I practically can't use this lighting. It allows me to notice an object, if the distance between it and me is about three to five centimeters. I sit down and go on thinking. There are just trifling things in my mind, nothing very optimistic.

* * *

Alexender A. Borovoi

In 1986, those who were at the Unit, or even just near the Unit, started terrible coughing. Practically all of them. I remember how many nights I slept, half-sitting, and almost coughed my bronchial tubes out of my body. And my condition was far from what could be called "the most difficult one." The first places in coughing were taken by two fellows among us. The first was a brilliant physicist, a very shy person. He looked really awful during his almost nonstop coughing attacks. There were no medicines to help him. It took great effort to persuade him to go and help us with calculations from Moscow. We managed to do it. I think that, with this, we saved his life. Now he is one of Russia's Academicians, but his cough left some unpleasant traces, as he confesses.

Another "champion" was a famous biophysicist, my friend. He didn't leave because there was nobody to replace him. As a result, he suffers constant and serious diseases. When I see him, I ask God to prolong his life. I was cured of all diseases, including Chernobyl ones, by my wife, as usual. Doctors still can't give any clear explanation of "Chernobyl coughing."

It's interesting. Will this coughing return when I get out of this damned darkness, or will it not? But I should get out first...

*　*　*

Can I estimate the dose I got? Only approximately. At this time, biophysicists and physicians can only approximate the danger from the inhalation of plutonium dust. I think one hour of work in this room is equal to a year of work in a maximum-dose field, permitted for professionals. Very approximately. But I still have some time.

My Chernobyl

* * *

I seem to have invented something! My students made me suffer a lot, but they taught me to be good on the uptake, although perhaps very slow. The electrical circuit for the lights, which is broken, is not the only one in the room. If they wanted to install detectors, there should be a switchboard connecting to other circuits. These circuits exist at the nuclear stations and have a reliable system that protects against defects and the loss of electrical power. We use them for our detectors. I must find this board and, with the help of the dim lighting on my watch, try to attach a searchlight to it. I am sure a searchlight is standing in a corner. To connect it to a 380-volt network with little or no lighting is a deadly trick. And if I had some light ...

I had a hope, though a small one.

The searchlight is very powerful. If I can get it to the door, I can illuminate the most terrible part of the way out.

* * *

In an hour and a half, I was at the medical post. I said to the duty dosimetrist that I had been in the other room, the clean room. He was almost sleeping and didn't check me up again. I washed. Or, to be more exact, practically scraped my skin over the next three days. And I coughed.

5. Robots

I was going to describe my first tour to the Station, to Unit 4. To tell what I felt during the fourteen-kilometer trip from Chernobyl to the Unit, how I looked at my dosimeter almost constantly, how I passed the famous Red Forest, and so on. But I stopped in time.

Practically all journalists and writers who were in Chernobyl described that journey. For many of them, their acquaintance with the accident was limited to this trip to the Station and back. You can imagine why so many creative powers and professional skills were put into these descriptions.

I can hardly add anything new to it.

I lay down my pen.

We came to the Unit; replaced lead protection, swearing heavily; did measurements; and went back. As I had supposed earlier, radiation in the Unit and in the ground contributed equally to the dose. We had to use "shadow" protection, and add sand and crushed stone to the soil.

Everyday life began.

Some episodes of it should be described, in my opinion.

* * *

In that time many newspapers were larded with headlines of the type: "Robot is walking around the Unit," "Robot constructors—to the heroes of Chernobyl," "Our modern robototechnics came to help," and others. That is why I was

My Chernobyl

surprised when the answer to my questions about where I could see our "modern robototechnics" was advice to roll with this robototechnics to ...

Generally, the male company gathered in Chernobyl and doing hard and dangerous work didn't shy from strong expressions. The national staff, mobilized to deal with the consequences of the accident, was ethnically mixed, especially in the military subunits. Of course, Russian was chosen as the language for international communication. And Russian curses took first place, indisputably. However, nobody was seriously upset by them, realizing that the expressions did not refer to the actual nearest relatives or the real bodies of the recipient. They simply referred to a stressful situation. On the other hand, if somebody used national expressions, he intended to offend an enemy, and at best, this ended in a fight. It reminded me of a story about a village where the residents didn't pay any attention to native expressions, but they were greatly concerned with foreign words. For example, saying the word *chemist* to a native left him only one response: to go and to burn the house of the offender.

We were used to curses, but we were shocked by the sincerity and depth of the curses addressed to robots. Or more precisely, to those who designed them.

It turned out that there were inventors out there who looked forward to saving the lives and health of workers in Chernobyl—and to get good money at the same time—using a new kind of robot of extraordinary construction. The authorities required immediate tests of the "savior," and those who were to be saved fought against this. Power and discipline won at last, and the robot was delivered to the Unit. The tests were to be done by Kurchatovers, who were taught how to operate the robot. The most sorrowful thing in this endeavor was that our colleagues were to ensure the safety of this robot—they signed a document—and the price was awfully high.

When the participants of the tests came back, they kept a mysterious silence. Only one answer followed all questions: "Everything was shot by TV camera and will be demonstrated to the authorities in the evening. You'll see everything yourself."

In the evening, we did see the film, if it is possible to give that name to a ten-minute recording. The authorities, members of the operative group, and, of course, constructors of the robot were present. One of the "creators" gave a short report about the great abilities of this wonderful mechanism. He didn't foresee what the film would reveal. Otherwise, the whole team of inventors would have been on their way to Kiev already.

In the beginning, a picture of the corridor where the tests were to be held appeared. This place was famous for its high radiation fields, which increased with the approach to the Unit. The robot was already in fighting trim; its operator and the other participants of these tests were behind the buttress. After short preparations, the robot rolled straight ahead on its wheels. It got about twenty feet, ran into an obstacle—a metal tube lying across the corridor—and stopped. I couldn't say that the tube was very big; its diameter wasn't more than five inches. In comparison with the robot, the obstacle looked minuscule, but nevertheless, the robot couldn't overcome the tube.

With the camera fixed on the robot, we saw two people in ordinary white jumpsuits and masks—who had obviously left their refuge, even though no one had foreseen that it would be necessary to enter areas of high radiation—run to the robot and carry it, with great difficulty, over the tube.

The robot continued on, but unfortunately, the way wasn't long again. In five feet it stopped. For some minutes the operator jerked and turned the handles on the operating board, but without any result. The robot moved neither forward nor backward. The camera recorded someone saying, "We shouldn't have affixed our signatures for this junk. Now we have to get into roentgens again. What did you do this for, Jura?"

Again, two white figures ran to the robot and turned it back. The operator manipulated the board, but the robot stood without moving. At last, the operator waved his hand in despair and stopped trying to bring life to the robot. Two or three minutes passed. And then, absolutely unexpectedly and absurdly waving its antennae and blinking its lamps, the robot turned the other way around, rolled along the corridor, made a grinding noise, and fell onto its back.

"Sound! Switch off the sound!" shouted the manager of these tests. But this shout was too late. Such masterly curses rushed upon the auditorium out of the TV speakers, that everyone involuntarily stood up. In such a ceremonial atmosphere, the demonstration ended.

The authorities asked only one question: "Did you get it?"

"Igor and Jura did."

* * *

That was the destiny of all the complex and expensive robots that were tested inside the Unit. They either got stuck in its ruins; or their electronics couldn't be operated in the immense radioactive fields, and the mechanisms "got crazy."

* * *

The first successfully working robot to actually help us in 1986 was ... a toy tank. It is difficult to believe this story, but it is absolutely true, and it is confirmed not only by the witnesses' stories, but by dozens of minutes of film.

Now, it is not an easy task to find out who was the first to decide to use the toy, but one of our team members, while in Kiev, bought this tank in the shop Everything for Children. He paid 12 rubles for it, about $5, according to the rate in those days. The tank was made of plastic, was about the size of a small telephone, and it had treads and a long cable that was attached to its operating unit. By this cable, power from the battery on the unit flowed to the electric motor on the tank, and the operating signal was transmitted.

The tank was able to move forward and backward, to turn and rattle, which imitated shooting. This last feature was useless in the Unit, but the previous two were used fully.

The tank was reconstructed. The cable was exchanged for a longer—about ten meters—and multichannel one, and we put a dosimeter, a thermometer, and a strong flashlight on it. With this, the tank could not only move, but also did primitive dosimetric and thermal exploring. It was an extraordinary "hunting dog," which could run on a lead before the "hunters" during the exploring and warn about danger. In spite of the fact that it had limited abilities, it honorably fulfilled its task and was easily decontaminated. The tank survived until the spring of 1987. After that, it couldn't be decontaminated any longer, and was buried in the block.

Thank you, small tank! (fig. 9)

Figure 9. The children's tank—the intelligence agent

* * *

Because of the absence of remote-controlled mechanisms that could work in case of accidents at nuclear facilities, a new institute was formed: Special Atom, aka Specatom. It was given the task to create the necessary robototechnics. This institute existed for several years, "ate" a lot of state money, and was shut down. No perceptible signs of its existence were left.

We had to start construction of robots for Shelter that wouldn't be burned in the radiation fields. Now they work at the block successfully enough. But this is for another time and another story (fig. 10).

At that time, only one type of "robot" truly existed and moved farther and farther in high fields and into dark, ruined rooms. These robots were people. By somebody's light hand they were called BIO-ROBOTS. This name stuck for a long time to those who worked inside and around the block.

Figure 10. Test of the robot on the ground in Chernobyl

6. Great Building

We are coming back to Shelter's creation, but now to the moments that took place before my eyes.

The end of the summer and the autumn of 1986 was the period of the Great Building.

Concrete plants were built in Chernobyl and in the Station's neighborhood. Huge machines milled compositions of concrete, sand, and crushed stone constantly. Every two minutes, at night and in daylight, powerful petrol tanks with roaring motors ran by the roads to the Station. They were followed by watering machines, which misted the dust in the air so that it wouldn't spread. Small Chernobyl houses, kept under the cover of fruit gardens and having lost their owners forever, trembled at the thunder of the passing vehicles.

At the Station, concrete was flowing like a river. Cranes of the Demagy worked day and night. Workers, engineers, and soldiers labored in four shifts, by sunlight and by searchlight.

At the same time, about ten thousand people were working at the ground.

Creation of Shelter was a task for a department that possessed giant building powers—the Ministry of Mechanical Engineering. A great Ministry, which studied the whole nuclear cycle, from the uranium extraction up to the nuclear weapons' creation to the burying of radioactive remains.

At meetings with the Government Commission Deputy Minister, chiefs of the departments of this Ministry, the leaders of building, reported about the thousands and thousands of cubic meters of laid concrete and the assemblage of great metallic constructions.

They were constantly urged to finish work on Shelter in time for the upcoming holiday—the sixty-ninth anniversary of the great October Revolution.

So, Shelter was growing before our eyes.

* * *

The first steps in its creation were building the walls and partitions that separated the destroyed Unit 4 from Unit 3.

These hermetic, defending-against-radiation walls were supposed to allow the personnel to work in normal conditions without fear of what would become an awful location in the future, when Unit 3 started working again.

Hurry up! Hurry up! Hurry up!

As a result, when our scouts succeeded in approaching these partitions a few years later, they turned out to be far from sealed. In some places, a man of average build could easily get into Unit 3 from Unit 4. Fortunately, plutonium dust was never able to sift through these holes. Thanks to the selfless work of my comrades, they managed to apply a special solution that acted as a glue on the dust. When constructions collapsed, the dust did not rise.

There were many other faults in the construction, but I won't speak about them. The worst thing was not that the people couldn't do their work properly in such extreme conditions. It was useless and sometimes criminal to want more from them. The worst thing was that those faults were glossed over because of fear of the authorities, and the general picture made to look much too optimistic. I could say a bad word about that tradition of arranging the end of a building's construction and the solving of all technical problems in time for political anniversaries.

From three sides of the approaches to the Unit, special defending walls were constructed. They ensured safety to some extent. These walls were called pioneers, but they were not at all small. About six meters high on the northern side, where a big mountain of destroyed walls and rubble from the building had formed—it was called the ruins—and about eight meters on the western and southern sides.

Three giant concrete steps enclosed the destroyed Unit on the northern side. Each was about twelve meters high. For their construction, a skeleton of metal beams was created. Then the internal space was filled with concrete, using the already mentioned concrete pumps, Putzmeisters.

The northern protective structure was called the cascade wall. The western wall was comparatively less. Windows were knocked out of the Unit, breaks were formed, and there was a part of the monolithic concrete rising above, like a lonely tooth. But still, it was a wall. It was decided to form big metallic constructions—"counterforces"—near the Unit, and then move them toward the Unit so that they could form the second metallic wall from the west. When it was built, it got the name counterforce wall (fig. 12).

To cover the Unit from above, what will serve as a base for the ceilings?

Three big steel beams, going west to east, were to hold all upper constructions. For successful fulfilment of their task, it was necessary to supply them with stable bases. The partial remains of the Unit, after its destruction by the accident, were to form those bases. You remember, we spoke about this before. Strengthening the old constructions, when there was no opportunity to come close, and we had to work almost blindly ... This was the task that stood before the workers. They poured for the foundation at a distance. The concrete flowed and flowed. Hundreds and then thousands of cubic meters poured into the lower floors of the building, into the darkness of radioactive rooms. And the workers continued to add concrete, to ensure maximum strength of the final construction.

Of course, they reported at the meetings of the Government Commission about the difficulties of pouring the concrete in this way, and nobody realized the real volume of the concrete.

Figure 11. Wall construction.

Figure 12. Western buttress wall

* * *

What were the Kurchatovers doing during this time? Why, during this tense period, was the most attention paid to their work, and why were they constantly required to make reports about it?

The reasons were absolutely different from one another, and I won't enumerate all of them.

The most important reason: constant anxiety felt by all, excepting a small group of professionals, that a nuclear reaction would flash in the destroyed Unit and a "second Chernobyl" would take place.

Our main efforts were directed at understanding where and in what condition the remaining fuel was, and then to take all the possible and impossible measures to ensure its safekeeping.

It was possible to explore the fuel by its radiation, by its giant—tens of thousands roentgen per hour—dose fields. But some difficulties existed.

First, radiation was absorbed in the thickness of the fuel itself, and in the walls and other materials as well. Because of this absorption, a layer of fuel of one meter shone just as much as a layer of five to seven centimeters. How do you count how many roentgen were in a layer?

Second, and this is the main thing, the procedure of exploring the fuel by its dose power implies the possibility of measuring the dose. But to measure it through the walls of the ruined Unit? Who knew the exact thickness of the materials in the ruins and the level by which the radiation was weakening? To measure, would we have to go directly into the rooms with this fuel? This would result in sickness and death.

The main chosen way of fuel exploring was a thermal one.

At this time, every ton of radioactive nuclear fuel radiated dozens of kilowatts of thermal power, at the expense of radionuclides' intensive decay. A volume of fuel equal to the size of a bucket gave off as much heat as hundreds of everyday electric heating appliances put together.

Alternately running and creeping into the remaining rooms and the ruins in the lower stores of the Unit, researchers tried to settle the means, displaying temperature and determining heat streams. Such methods of heat location helped to ascertain, for example, a large fuel congestion that had penetrated into the room under the reactor.

From above, in the former Central Hall, devices called buoys were settled with the help of helicopters and cranes (fig. 13).

Figure 13. Buoy No. 14 is installed in the destroyed reactor

These devices looked like usual river buoys that serve as orientation points for vessels. But these buoys were just stuffed inside with equipment. Standing among the ruins and the materials thrown from the helicopters, they registered heat streams, temperature, speed of air moving, and dose fields. All information was transmitted by cables to a central control panel. Periodically, workers broke those cables and another buoy fell silent. The last of them fell silent in October of 1986.

* * *

In the morning and during the day, I fulfilled different tasks for the operative group authorities. I went to the Unit with my coworkers, processed measurement results, solved the problems of plutonium thrown out of the reactor. And in the evenings, I was to be present at the Government Commission's meetings.

Alexender A. Borovoi

I would sit in the farthest corner and observe the generals, the big institutes' authorities, and even ministers who were making their reports for the Commission. The Commission's members changed periodically. Some of them, "having got their roentgens," left for Moscow. Others, having come to their senses, solved urgent Moscow problems and returned to Chernobyl. The Chairman left sometimes also. At those times, everybody felt more relaxed and the meetings passed more quickly.

I listened to the disputes that often arose and sometimes wanted to express my opinion, but nobody was interested in it.

I had only one way to influence events when it seemed absolutely necessary—to convince my chiefs, and they in their turn would make a report to the Government Commission or try to convince the Chairman of a necessary working regimen.

* * *

Time flew. Workers continued to create Shelter, and more concrete flowed into uncertainty. Military helicopters hanging over the Unit registered dose power from the height of two hundred meters every day. Physicists tried to get information about the fuel.

So "X hour," which determined my destiny in many aspects, was prepared little by little.

7. Two Hours

The day started quite nice. A cool and sunny autumn day in October of 1986. I walked along Chernobyl's narrow lanes, far from the main roads. The constant hum of cars hardly broke through the gardens. I had hoped to relax after the previous day's hard work at the Unit, sitting in headquarters and processing measurement results. And to think over a very important question, one which gave us no peace for many days, up to the very end. But a man supposes, and destiny ...

* * *

In a few hours, I found myself on the second floor. Some minutes earlier, Academician Legasov came into our headquarters and led me to Chairman Scherbina's office. Scherbina didn't waste time on greetings.

"Do you know that radiation above the Unit increased by four times? Didn't know yet? Pilots of the helicopters registered this fact today. And your physicists registered temperature increases in the lower rooms, under the exploded reactor. Why nobody reported the fact to me immediately, we will find out later. We have no time now. The activity of air filters at the ground increased by dozens of times.

"It seems that an uncontrollable chain nuclear reaction has started inside the Unit. You are to learn the reason. Quickly and thoroughly. I can give you only two hours. If you cannot prove that this is not a nuclear hazard, we will raise the alarm and lead the people out of the plant. Thousands of people are working there today. I can't give you more time.

Alexender A. Borovoi

"Until you fulfill the task and report personally to me or Academician Legasov, you shouldn't talk about nuclear hazard. It is usual staff work. Urgent work, but a usual one. Any help will be rendered immediately."

I return to the headquarters. An unknown man follows me. He shows me his documents; he is an officer of the Committee of State Security (KGB). He tells me insistently to sign every piece of paper, every list of calculations, and then to give everything to him. Again and again, he warns me of responsibility.

* * *

If you have little time but you have resources for solving a problem, you move in several ways at once. If you have enough time but your resources are limited, you form a consecutive chain of tasks that need to be fulfilled to let you reach the final point.

If you have neither time nor resources, you have only one thing to do: hope you are lucky.

I was lucky to get resources. I don't know what was reported from the Government Commission to the operative group, but in a few minutes, many Kurchatovers were mobilized to help me. Some of them went to the Station to control the situation with the filters. Others went to the pilots of the helicopters to get the documents from the onboard equipment. The smartest and most diplomatic people were sent to the workers, so that in exclusive, private talks they could learn about ... But we'll speak about this later.

Finally, some people were sent to the Unit with portable instruments to take samples of air on short-living products of decay—a sure sign of a CNR—in all possible places.

To tell the truth, I didn't believe even for a minute in nuclear hazard. More so because I already had the answer for one of the Chairman's questions.

Why had the temperature begun to increase in the lower rooms of the Unit, near the reactor's shaft?

We had discussed this problem the previous day, and almost everybody agreed with me that the reason was the concrete that had been poured into the Unit. If earlier, the air could go freely through the corridors and rooms, taking heat radiated by nuclear fuel with it, the concrete now created obstacles to this natural ventilation. The fuel was warming and the temperature increasing.

It was a simple explanation, and already the first estimations given were, as I had thought, fantastic figures of the poured concrete's quantity. Hundreds of cubic meters! (Later, it became clear that the real quantity was thousands of it.) That's why we didn't hurry to report that temperature rise, and decided to clear up this delicate question with the workers.

The "diplomats," returning quickly enough from Building Management, reported that our supposition that the new concrete had begun to impede the air flow that cooled the fuel was confirmed—unofficially.

The situation with the increase of air-filter activity was also easily explained. Somebody had been sharp enough to move the assemblies for air sampling, situated at a minimal distance from the ruins, closer to the road, where there was a constant stream of truck traffic that lifted heavy dust into the air. In their new place, the filters measured not the activity release from the Unit, but something uncertain that was most likely also connected with the concrete.

The traffic volume was so high, it wasn't surprising that the air filters' activity had increased by dozens of times. It was more surprising it hadn't increased by hundreds. The assemblies had been moved, but no one—neither those who'd moved the assemblies nor those who changed the filters—had reported it. Thank God, it wasn't done by the Kurchatovers.

As for the third problem, the readings of the helicopters' equipment increasing by four times—we had to work hard on that one.

Every day, according to the program called Gulls, a helicopter did some dosimetric measurements, flying on a certain course over the Unit at the height of two hundred meters. When it was just above Shelter's roof, dose power during previous days consisted of 12-10-10 R/h. Suddenly, today, it was about 40 R/h!

Dosimetric instruments were situated outside the helicopter's cabin. Their readings were transmitted to the onboard computer, and the result was displayed on a screen. Nobody in Chernobyl knew what operations electronics did with the transmitted data. The inventors of this equipment were far away, and it would take too much time to find them. That's why I had to sit and count myself.

I won't tire the reader with my computations. I'll just say that I filled sheet after sheet, constantly making mistakes and deleting the results, being excited as I had never been in my life that—although I was awfully behind in time—I was finally able to get to the right road. The calculations convinced me that the readings of the onboard computer should be divided by a coefficient that was equal to four!

I call the military pilots.

"Did a new crew fly today?"

"Yes, a new shift arrived yesterday."

"Can I speak to the pilot who was replaced? Is he here yet?"

"You are lucky, he is just getting into his car. We'll call him."

"I understand you," the pilot says. "Yes, yes. Of course, we divided it by the coefficient. The inventors of this equipment calculated it for us. Yes, it equals four. Why didn't we give it to the other shift? We gave it. I remember this exactly. We gave and made entries in the journals. Maybe they had no time to read them carefully. They were woken up very early today."

The new shift assured me that nobody gave them anything, that they had nothing of the kind. I didn't look into this matter. I had neither the time nor the desire. The pilots were sent to us from Afghanistan, after serving in continuous battle. And they came to Chernobyl at once, fulfilling tasks that nobody envied.

* * *

Scherbina didn't look into details either. He listened to me attentively, thought for a while, and then, looking into my eyes, said very clearly: "I am not a scientist and I can't repeat your calculations. And I can't believe fully in such a combination of accidental matters. People are working at the Station and I am responsible for their lives. I can't believe in your report. I am sorry. You are to present unconditional and absolutely clear proofs. I am not going to abolish the emergency situation. I give you two or three more hours."

In answer to my timid words that our teams had discovered no signs of short-living products of decay, he barked, "Only for this reason I am prolonging the term."

Silence. As I was walking toward the door, one idea, feasible at first sight, flashed in my mind.

* * *

Three hours flew. Legasov and Scherbina leaned over the table looking at the still-moist photos, pictures of the instrument board of a helicopter and a full set of dosimeters:

- Soviet—four types
- ORIENT, a Japanese production
- PENDIX, made in the United States

Readings of these dosimeters were limited to 8–10 R/h.

"Our workers," Legasov said, "hung above the Unit in the helicopter. You can see this by the onboard readings. The height is two hundred meters. And you can see the readings of different kinds of dosimeters. We can't speak about those 40 R/h readings. The division coefficient proved correct—four."

"Yes," the Chairman agreed unwillingly. "But still, do check it once again."

Flights continued the next day, and one more day after. They changed helicopters, onboard dosimeters, repeated the experiment with foreign dosimeters. Everything proved correct.

* * *

The KGB officer took those crumpled but signed papers and left. I never saw him again.

My Chernobyl

* * *

I was present at an ordinary meeting of the Government Commission in my favorite corner. I practically hadn't slept the previous three nights. I hardly went to bed when the continuous coughing began, going into asthmatic attacks. The meeting seemed incredibly boring, some deliveries, metal supplies. Then there was a nice pause. It turned out that I hadn't only fallen asleep, I had fallen into the aisle. Thank my neighbors, they not only picked me up by my padded jacket, but also put me back in my initial position. I looked at the Chairman with horror. Scherbina said nothing, only shook his head. Some time passed, an interesting question was discussed, and suddenly the Chairman said, addressing me for the first time in all those months, "I would like to know the opinion of Science, if it has got up already."

8. Apples

During this period, I saw the Chairman in different situations and different roles. Most often, he played a hard and a harsh person. Others were afraid of him and tried to avoid his eyes more than was necessary. But the circumstances and his great responsibility didn't incline him to an especially good nature. I was just surprised when I saw Scherbina quickly get to the hearts of new and ever newer problems, in spite of his not at all young years.

Situations were different.

* * *

More than a hundred thousand people were evacuated from the Zone by that autumn. Livestock was also led out. Villages were empty, and houses looked out with dead eyes. Unharvested grain was left in the fields, and an immense quantity of field mice fussed about the dried spikes. In the evenings, dozens of owls began flying over the crops, looking like plane squadrons coming in for bombings. Various fruits rotted on the ground in the gardens. Late apples were still on the trees, and my colleagues, coming back from the Unit, picked them and ate with pleasure. I didn't eat, not because of a fear of radioactivity—when the apples were peeled, they were quite edible—but because of my old hatred toward even just a little sour fruits.

* * *

Early one morning, we arrived by helicopter in one of the abandoned villages. We were to take ground samples and bring them back for analysis. In spite of the sunny morning and the beauty of the autumn forest, which began right behind the last house, there was a constant weight in hearts, as if we were in a cemetery.

We were finishing our work when a strange procession came out a nearby house. There was an old woman with a cat in her hands, and she was followed by another old woman and an old man, whom she helped along. We were absolutely shocked. According to what we knew, the territory around the Zone was solitary for many kilometers. The first thing that came to my mind was that a military unit that was helping to evacuate the village had forgotten to lead these old people out, either because of some oversight or because of hurry.

I rush toward them, and the first question I ask is not very clever: "Why are you here?"

The old man answers. "We were born here, and your military people didn't find us. We hid in the forest. Nobody could find us in the forest, even the Germans during the war. They had very good specialists with dogs, tried to find us, but failed. It was much easier with your soldiers. We passed absolutely free of their posts by using the paths. We went out of the Zone, went to confession, and came back." He speaks with pride.

"Tell us," he goes on. "But don't be afraid, tell the truth. Will we live until the winter with this radiation? Or will we die earlier? We don't care much about death, but we should know how much firewood we should store, and what about provisions? We came out now only for one reason—to ask somebody, and you are working with instruments. Tell us, please."

I feel a strong tickle in my throat, but not because of Chernobyl's hot particles.

"Radiation is not high here," I answer, "and the level will fall quickly enough. You got your main dose in the first weeks after the accident. But even this dose is far from a fatal one. How old are you?"

The old man turns out to be about eighty years old, and the old women are over seventy.

"Well, you see," I say, "you have got enough diseases during your life. Only God can decide what will be the reasons for your death, but radiation will not be the reason."

"Can I let the animal walk on the ground?" asks the woman with the cat. "It is difficult to carry it, but I am afraid of its legs. Will they be burned, will it become a freak?"

"No, nothing will happen to it, you may let it down."

"What can we eat from the trees? Can we eat apples?"

"Yes, you can, but first peel them."

"Eat an apple," says the old man.

I pick an apple and eat it. Oh, my God! I have never eaten a sourer apple in my life. I have cramps in my cheekbones, but I remember their long way, their walk to the church and back, the way through the forest thicket, dozens of kilometers long, this old man led by the old woman, and the cat ... And I am not only eating the apple, I am smiling at the same time. The apple is over at last.

"Eat some more," the old man says. I am eating ...

My colleagues, having run up to us and knowing perfectly well my dislike of apples, look around as if admiring the scenery.

Our time is up.

My Chernobyl

We spoke to the pilots and left those old people all the canned food and chocolate from our emergency rations.

* * *

In the evening, I waited till there were no visitors in Scherbina's office and asked the secretary to let me in for three minutes. I told the Chairman about those old people and that I advised them to stay in spite of all instructions and rules. Scherbina looked at me with eyes red from sleeplessness.

"They escaped the German soldiers, and ours drove them into the forest. They asked for their right to die in their own homes? How can we refuse? Who can do it? Let them live there. Have you any more suggestions?"

"There is a military unit not far from this place. Is it possible to order them to send their field kitchen to this village once a day? Just to feed them. The food will be clear, and the external radiation is very small."

"All right. You may go."

Leaving the office, I heard him asking for the connection with the military authorities.

1987 and Further

1. When I Began to Write This Book

I am flying over the United States, Albuquerque to Phoenix to Washington. Flight of fancy! Up to 1989, I couldn't imagine I would fly over this great country, that I would even get abroad. The few invitations from abroad that had come for me had had only one destiny: an ordinary clerk decorated them with the inscription "There is no necessity in this tour" and added the document to the file. My tours didn't move farther than this file. But in 1989, the Minister declared that everything concerning Chernobyl was open information and could be told at conferences, could be printed in magazines and books. That was in the summer, and already in the winter the International Atomic Energy Agency (IEAE) invited me to Vienna as an expert on Chernobyl. One invitation followed another. Everything would be very good ... except for my English.

Its condition was absolutely pitiful.

At one of the conferences, after my vain efforts to understand the reporters, I vented my irritation on a gentle and polite Indian scientist. He came up to me during an interval and started to twitter something melodious.

"You are fully mistaken," I said, "if you think I can understand something. I understand not more than a clever dog. At the initial stage of its training."

At any rate, I wanted to express these thoughts. After my little speech, the man thanked me a lot and said, as far as I could understand, that he really wanted to study radiation influence upon big animals.

Alexender A. Borovoi

This episode finished me.

I decided to study English seriously. And now, when everybody wants to share his experience in how English should be studied, I possibly will serve a happy exception, because I want to tell how English should not be studied.

You shouldn't study English independently.

You shouldn't start studying English if you are far over fifty.

You shouldn't study it at night.

Oral repetition of English phrases while working in radioactive rooms can form a wrong opinion of your sanity.

You shouldn't be surprised when a person you are talking to will not guess what English words you know and will choose others when answering your question.

You shouldn't ...

Only one thing consoled me. The famous French scientist, Professor Pier Pelleren, having worked with us inside Shelter for more than two weeks in 1991, a person greatly respected by me, studied Russian using my methods.

I should say that he hadn't any noticeable results.

Four years of studying have passed and now, sitting in the plane, I am checking my English on Gary Dunbar, vice president of the firm LATA. Gary is a good friend of mine, and only this fact and Gary's natural patience give him the ability to listen to my Chernobyl stories. Within an hour, he grows noticeably sad. But then a happy idea of how to avoid complete exhaustion comes to my friend's mind.

"Alexander," he says, "it would probably be better if you were to translate these stories into normal English and type them. Then I would be able to read your stories without hurry and at rest. I'll even help you in organizing this."

The idea catches me. It is like a last drop overflowing a

My Chernobyl

bowl. So, from time to time, on trains from Moscow to Kiev and Kiev to Moscow; in the evenings instead of my English studies; at boring conferences; secretly, I begin to write this book.

2. Elephant Leg

On the 8th of December of 1989, in *Pravda*, which at that time was the main newspaper of our country, an article titled "What are people doing in the sarcophagus?" was printed. It contained pictures, and so a photo of Elephant Leg was printed for the first time. The Leg was a giant radioactive stalactite formed by the frozen lava. Later, its photos appeared in different publications, in color and black-and-white, made with different exposures and lighting.

The Elephant Leg was worth this glory, because it made us work very hard in 1986–1987. And one time it hardly avoided being the cause of a real tragedy.

It was discovered in one of the rooms (building mark 6m) in the autumn of 1986. To see the Elephant Leg, one had to get through a hole, narrow enough, in any case, for my size. In a few meters, this hole led you into a service corridor. There was a door in this corridor on the right, the door of a room that was highly suitable for us for our thermal exploring. As it turned out later, the room was located down from and to the side of the main lava flows. There were many tubes in this room, and it was very hot there, about 40° C (104° F). But still, the dose power was low enough that it was quite accessible. On the left, the corridor broadened, and there, in the distance, a big black drop with a smooth surface stood out in all its beauty. Coolness and radiation (8000 R/h) reigned around this drop (fig. 14).

My Chernobyl

Figure 14. The Elephant Leg

At once, we asked a lot of questions, and the first one was: What material from the accident formed this Elephant Leg?

The material looked like lead because of its dim glittering. So, was the lead that was supposed to take the heat of the nuclear fuel discovered at last? If so, then not in vain was it thrown into the burning reactor. And all the accusations hurled at the originators of the idea of using lead, that the lead had just evaporated and contaminated the surrounding territory, were wrong.

The Government Commission's orders were short and clear: take photos, samples, and make a detailed analysis.

* * *

Very few people, excepting Kurchatovers, know what difficult and important tasks our photographers and videographers fulfilled in Chernobyl. They went with the explorers into the darkness of the destroyed Unit. They burned in radiation fields, but worried not about their health, only about their equipment. They covered their cameras with lead so that the film wouldn't be spoiled by a fog from the radiation, brought devices for lighting, and carried all this heavy equipment sometimes to the height of a twenty-story building, running in some places. Other members of the group, after leaving the Unit, had the opportunity to wash and have a little rest, but for the photographers, a new and responsible task began: to develop and print the photos. Then there was the decontamination and repairing of their equipment. And the next morning, there was a new task from the Government Commission and a new tour to the Station. Or taking photos from the air, leaning out of the helicopter's hatch, hanging above the reactor's shaft at the height of two hundred meters.

The photographers were led by Valentin Obodzinsky. He was the first to take photos of the Elephant Leg, but in black-and-white. After the Government Commission saw them, there was another order: make colored photos. But Obodzinsky wasn't in the operative group by that time. His health had reduced to such a critical level, our authorities ordered him to go to Moscow and sent a substitute. So, there appeared a new person in our group. He had never been in Chernobyl before, and he not only had to visit the Unit, but had to creep in the most difficult way to the Elephant Leg and take high-quality colored photos of it the day after his arrival.

* * *

Try to imagine the following picture. One of the comparatively clean rooms of the Unit. (Clean, in our slang, meant cleaned-up from radioactivity, deactivated.) Gray concrete walls, two tables covered with polyethylene. There are instruments on the tables and a mess of cables on the concrete floor. At the entrance of this room, dividing it, there is a bench. Everybody entering the room sits down on the bench and puts clean—or, to be more correct, cleaner—shoes on, and then comes into the room itself. We are discussing something intensely, and at that moment the light fades. The situation is not new—the workers chopped the power cable again. Everybody is in great hurry. The holidays are coming, inevitably, but Shelter is very far from its finish.

The light is switched off, but we have miner's torches, and in their beams I see that a very good but absent-minded fellow has come into the room but didn't change his shoes. While the others remind him, with pleasure, of our routine rules, anxiety originates deep inside me. This fellow, experienced in walking around the Unit, was to accompany the photographer who had just arrived from Moscow to the Elephant Leg and to ensure dosimetric control. He went with DP-5, and the photographer brought expensive Japanese equipment. Of course, the room is dark, but it is lighted enough that I would notice the photographer. He is not there.

"What have you managed to photograph?" I ask cautiously.

In the light of the torches, I see the man's growing absolutely pale, even white.

"I led him," he says, "to the room on the right, the hot room with a small dose, crept for the additional searchlight, came back to the fellows, chattered ... and forgot, quite forgot, that he is there ... below. He is waiting, can't go out himself ..."

Absolute silence fell instantly. I think the same picture was before everybody's eyes. The man, drenched with sweat, is sitting in a small room and waiting. He has just made a terrible start for a beginner. He is not a professional and must be very frightened. He is waiting, but nobody is coming. He has to go out somehow; he cannot wait in uncertainty and unbearable heat. And then the light is switched off. Even a person who knows the way well can hardly find the hole through which they came. The photographer stands up and goes, walks along a normal corridor, toward cool silence. Toward agonizing death.

We need only an instant to imagine all this.

I want to stand up, but my legs have become numb and can't hold me. I am like a drunk. I let him down in this decisive moment. But there are people who didn't. I am just trying to make the first step, but already a figure, with a sob and a wheeze from his burned lungs, disappears at the end of the corridor.

He ran in time. The photographer had just come into the corridor. When he saw a man with a miner's torch on his head getting out the hole, he cried and started to beat his savior around the head with the expensive Japanese camera.

In the evening, all members of the operative group gathered in the Gynecology. There were no announcements and only one short speech. One of us stood up and said: "Let him go. We won't work with the person who forgot about his colleague." Then everybody left the room.

*　*　*

The photographer's troubles didn't end with this incident. The next day he had to fly by helicopter and, as already described, photograph the Unit. Of course, he tried his best, but there was mainly sky in the developed photos. A week passed, and the photographer changed greatly. We had to hold him by his tail so that he wouldn't forget and go into a high radioactive fields, or worse, fall out of the helicopter.

We worked many years with him.

* * *

Our efforts to take samples of the Elephant Leg's substance failed one by one. First, researchers constructed an automated cart and put an electric drill on it. The cart was able to get to the stalactite, but the drill couldn't bore holes in it. The substance was too hard.

The next try was done by the military, which observed the diffident efforts of the scientists with reproach. I wasn't present at this incident, but according to witnesses, the military approach was done in an attack style. Nobody could gather their wits fast enough when a brave officer ran to the Elephant Leg and started to beat it with an axe. The results were minimal, excepting his immediate removal from Chernobyl.

After several encroachments that left the Leg intact, we finally managed to take samples of the substance for analysis. The analysis showed no signs of lead, but there existed a peculiar glasslike mass that contained the whole set of nuclear fuel radionuclides. So, for the first time we came across the most original substance, born in the devil kitchen of the accident. This was the substance we called lava.

* * *

Alexender A. Borovoi

In the spring of 1987, the question of studying the Elephant Leg's substance arose again. We had information only about the surface. What was inside it? Of course, nobody seriously hoped to find the long-awaited lead, but it was necessary to understand the inner structure and contents of the lava mass.

* * *

Shift authorities of the operative group consisted of two people—a manager and a scientific supervisor. As the latter, I came to Chernobyl on March 2, 1987. In this first shift as well as the others, I was lucky to have good managers. They were talented and experienced engineers and good friends. In March, it was Alexey Borokhovich, who differed from the others only in his great knowledge in the sphere of dosimetry and a boundless energy for dealing with management. He reproached me for a long time when I gave, without hesitation, one of our reports to some military men.

"They use them to report to their authority, presenting them as their own achievements, and sometimes they don't even thank us," Borokhovich said indignantly.

"What can I do?" I asked. "We are working together. I can't refuse to give this to them."

"Of course, you are to give, but do it using your brains. The military department is awfully rich. Let them help with our needs. Let me show you next time how to do this."

I agreed. The handing of the next report was done behind shut doors and lasted for a long time. At last, both negotiating sides exited, everyone smiling with satisfaction. To my question—What goods had he managed to get?—Borokhovich answered secretly, "You'll see this evening."

In the evening, I was coming to our living quarters.

I should say that in this time we were living in a separate two-story building, with our own cars and trucks, warehouses, and a nice medical post on the ground floor with constant dosimetric and medical controls. Generally, we lived well, better than both before and after in Chernobyl, and all this was due to Borokhovich's energy.

As I neared the building, I saw at once a big trailer and a lively chain of the Kurchatovers, who were passing some packets one to another into our warehouse.

"Here!" exclaimed the last man in this chain. "We have been unloading this for an hour already. The military people sent this to us. For one report." He spoke with pride.

"And what is in the packets?"

"Pants. Three thousand pairs."

"Isn't that too many for thirty people?" I asked hesitantly. "They may think that we don't behave very bravely at the Unit."

But the general enthusiasm didn't allow anybody to share my apprehensions.

* * *

When the question of studying the Elephant Leg came up again, the manager of the operative group rose like a wall against additional irradiation of people. We had to invent remote technology to do the sampling. Having suffered for some evenings trying to come up with something, we finally hit on an idea. We decided to shoot this monster with guns, and to do it so that the bullets could get one into another, and we could then take samples from its depth.

Alexender A. Borovoi

First, though, nobody wanted to give us the weapons. Military men sent us to the militia organizations, and from there we were sent to KGB, and from KGB we were sent to the militia again. Our importunity and the fact that a good sniper, Captain Soroko, worked in the militia at that time helped us a lot. He decided to put this unusual shooting exercise into practice himself.

There is a videotape, used in a BBC film, about the shooting. It was done successfully, exactly according to our outlined plan, and it got us samples of substance from the depth of the Elephant Leg. Samples that fully proved the initial analysis, that Leg's substance was a glasslike lava.

3. Books and Photos

A deep night. I am sitting in the working room of my Chernobyl flat. These word combinations seem very strange—Chernobyl flat, working room. The 1986 dream of my own bed had become reality. But, on the other hand, one can't live only in a bed for eight years.

In 1988, when our operative group was reformed into the Complex Expedition at the Kurchatov Institute and some building units were given to us, a period of great building began. Some separate constructions inside the Unit were strengthened, Machine Hall was decontaminated from radioactive obstructions, rooms for work were won back out of the Unit. Using the workers, we managed to re-equip an old school building in Chernobyl into a modern laboratory block. Entrances to a five-story building, which had started to be built in Chernobyl before the accident, were also finished. It was taken by the Kurchatovers.

My colleagues live in neighboring flats. Not, of course, in such a splendid condition as mine, but still in separate rooms. It is very convenient. We can discuss any urgent questions at any time, night or day; but at the same time, it's not so convenient. Ideas come to my colleagues more often in the night and I still can't give up the habit of sleeping during those hours.

Usually in the period between eleven and one o'clock, there is a knocking at my door and somebody is asking, "Are you asleep already?"

How can I refuse to listen to a person who has invented an

absolutely genius method to fix the counter used in a just-bored hole? Is it possible to disappoint him with the fact that the room into which the hole was bored turned out to be uninteresting, and we don't need to fix the counter at all?

Of course not. First of all, I must evaluate this invention, and then gradually lead the talk so that he comes to the conclusion that there is no need to fix the counter and he can go to bed, all calmed down. The only thing is that there is then little time left to sleep.

There are no visitors tonight. And I don't want to sleep. I am going through the books about Chernobyl, the photos, lying on the table. Looking through them, I give absolute freedom to my memory. I don't consider chronology of events or their importance. Just the light flashes before my eyes, some picture appears, and my past surrounds me ...

* * *

The book *Chernobyl: Five Difficult Years* is on top. It is a slim book. My first impression: one could have written more about five years of the work at Chernobyl, even if describing only our Institute's work.

I prepared a chapter about Shelter for this publication. I didn't write much, but everything was shortened significantly. Nobody is interested in it? I think that is not true. The whole edition sold out very quickly.

How did the idea for this book come about? I'll try to remember...

Legasov invited a small group of Kurchatovers to the office of the vice chairman of the Government Commission. He showed us the plan for the future book about the recovery from the accident. Every department was to write its own volume—military, medical, workers, science...

"No lesson of Chernobyl should be forgotten. Everything should serve people. We paid too high a cost for them."

A dozen volumes were prepared, but the entirety of interesting information was not presented in them. The volumes covered maybe only one-third. The volumes themselves are still unpublished.

This slim book is the final result.

* * *

I am looking at one of the illustrations which represents the dose fields on the roofs of Units 3 and 4.

Spring of 1987. Roof covered with snow.

How I hated those tours to the roofs, situated at the height of many dozens of meters! We had to get there by a fire ladder, as a rule, its slippery steps coated with ice, with an inconvenient dosimeter on our backs. All my life I tried to avoid sports lessons and was afraid of heights. And that time, both aversions were combined into a pleasant combination. But it is necessary to climb to roofs; they are not fully decontaminated from the radioactive fragments. We have to go there to outline a plan for their decontamination, and so I play the sorry part of a mountain climber.

I am standing behind the buttress of a wall. Radiation is less here than in the open place where Legasov is standing. Already for two or three minutes, I have been trying to convince him to come to the refuge, mostly because the view is equally bad in both places. Legasov waves me away. He is standing and looking like a tourist, observing the fragments of unknown origin covered with snow. What can I do? I can't use physical power, and he is ignoring my words.

Fortunately, a military man with stars, which are drawn in ink on the shoulders of his insulated jacket, appears near me on the roof. The stars have blurred, but I could distinguish his rank: major. Since the Academician is wearing a plain insulated jacket without any distinguishing signs and he looks young, his face covered with a respirator, I try to use the situation to its best advantage.

I point to Legasov and say, "Major, is that your soldier? Why didn't you instruct your people? They are burning here in vain. What disorder you have!"

The Major swallows the lure at once.

He orders the Academician to leave the roof immediately, with such convincing words in such a strong and husky voice, that the member of the Government Commission obeys immediately to avoid a brawl.

"These military men get out of hand," Legasov complains when we reach the ground at last.

"They have no choice," I answer with malice. "The reinforcements are absolutely ignorant."

* * *

Not long before his death, I met Academician Legasov in a corridor of the main building. He had been ill for the last months, didn't work on Chernobyl, looked very bad. To my question about his health, Legasov answered quietly, "How can a man feel without a liver?"

And I remembered that damned roof.

My Chernobyl

* * *

A book with a black cover. A splendid publication in English. It was sent as a present to me by a journalist. *Ablaze: The Story of Chernobyl,* by Piers Paul Read.

I opened the book and looked first at the chapter concerning the Complex Expedition (which I will explain shortly), beginning on page 442. There were several mistakes on each page. The main data, dates, names were mixed. I didn't read any more, leaving it for a future time.

* * *

A photo. Workers at Chernobyl—Chernobylers—have orders conferred on them.

In these years, government rewards had prestige. They gave not only moral satisfaction, but also perceptible material goods. The right to move ahead in the line for a living place and a car, to get a pass to a sanatorium, etc.

The stream of rewards rushed onto people who had any connection to Chernobyl exceeded all expectations. Not only those who worked in the Zone and near it were rewarded. Those who helped them, working far from Chernobyl, were rewarded also. The total number of the rewarded, according to my evaluations, was tens of thousands of people.

Not a single Kurchatover was conferred orders or medals.

To the direct question—What was the reason for such injustice?—the clerks gave typical answers. They rolled their eyes and said that "they" decided not to reward the workers of some institutes, because these institutes were morally

Alexender A. Borovoi

responsible for the accident. Nobody was interested in an actual person, or the high heroism and courage that person displayed. It wasn't important that he had no connection to the causes of the accident. So, in the first place, honors were not based on services, but on belonging to a certain organization. (Extend this logic to where a person lives or his nationality. The accident took place in Ukraine, so Ukrainian shouldn't be rewarded.) This system, in my opinion, devalued the Chernobyl rewards.

Legasov was treated especially poorly. On the eve of the publication of the list of rewarded people, everybody was absolutely sure he would be awarded, with other chosen ones, the high Soviet reward of Hero Star, Hero of Russia. Alexandrov, director of the Institute, congratulated Legasov in public at the Institute. And in the morning, his name wasn't on the list. It was crossed out. There was a lot of talk and rumors about this. Then the Chernobylers decided that this was done by Gorbachev, who disliked the famous Academician. The image of the ex-president, firmly formed by people, was in absolute conformity with this action.[3]

* * *

One more photo. Laboratory in Chernobyl. A famous American scientist is in my office, and he is smiling joyfully. Looking at the photo, I remember the events that preceded this meeting, and smile also.

---

[3] On September 20, 1996, the president of Russia signed the decree for the posthumous rewarding of the rank of Hero of Russia for Academician Legasov, for "the courage and heroism shown during elimination of the Chernobyl accident."

My Chernobyl

In the morning, on the Moscow-Kiev train, I am leaving my compartment when I see an agitated and distressed foreigner. After a few efforts, I managed to figure out the following. He and his wife arrived from the United States the previous evening. The wife got sick on the plane and ate nothing. Right after the flight, they went to the railway station and had no time to eat. They wanted to eat on the train, but that turned out to be impossible. There is no restaurant, no bar, on the train, and the steward was just throwing up his hands. Either he couldn't understand, or he had no food except for tea and sugar. The American's wife hasn't eaten for two days. What to do?

I was traveling with a friend, and we both were experienced travelers on Soviet railways. That's why a full plate of sandwiches and pies, prepared by our wives, was standing in all its beauty before the American lady in five minutes. The husband tried to foist money on us, and when we refused, he thanked us for a long time. An accidental meeting of no significance.

Some days later, a member of the Foreign Department visited me. This all took place in a time when any contact with foreigners was strictly limited and controlled. This member said there was a decision about my upcoming meeting with an American scientist of high status. The program was already outlined. I was to talk only within the limits of this program, and within the time limit. To answer the questions in this and that way, and to avoid asking my own questions.

I became angry and asked, "How should I greet him? Should I, according to our leaders' example, embrace and kiss him?"

The member's response was very serious. No, I shouldn't kiss him. I shouldn't embrace him either. The maximum I

Alexender A. Borovoi

could do—shake his hand.

***

A whole company gathered in my office the day of the visit: the member of the Foreign Department, his assistant, a photographer, and me. The door opened, and there was an interpreter and—my fellow railway traveler. Apparently, he had not been well instructed, because the American opened his arms as he entered my office, came to me, and embraced me. Of course, I embraced him also, and said to the member over the American's shoulder: "Please make a note that it was he who started this."

***

After the Ministry ordered that all works on Chernobyl were opened, we met dozens of delegations. But nobody embraced me anymore.

***

The clock is ticking. I can't fall asleep. One more packet with photos is lying on my table. It is bitter for me to open it. They are photos of my friends who died. Everybody had one reason. No, not radiation sickness. Heart. It was difficult for hearts to bear the Chernobyl of '86–'88. Constant stresses, constant lack of sleep, constant need for self-preservation.

***

My Chernobyl

A lengthy talk with foreign journalists is coming to its end. There were and there will be many such talks. I am waiting for the inevitable question. Today, this question is asked at the very end. Sometimes it is asked in the middle, very rarely in the beginning, but it is asked without fail. A journalist with spectacles comes closer to me and says, "Tell me, please, why did Academician Legasov commit suicide?"

Everybody thinks that, working with him in Chernobyl and in Moscow, I must know some "real truth." But the "real truth" consists of only three words:

"I don't know."

* * *

The question of whether to commit suicide or not is a question of the inner world, a question of the condition of a man's soul, and this awful choice cannot be explained by external reasons.

* * *

His office in the Institute.

I was asked to check his papers and belongings for radioactivity before giving them to his family. They are lying on his table, covered with polyethylene.

I read somewhere that all of Pierre and Marie Curie's belongings in the Curie Museum in Paris are radioactive. If you level your counter to them, it starts tapping, and this will last practically forever.

I level my counter to Legasov's things lying on the table. It starts tapping. It is throbbing, like a child's heart.

4. October 13, 1987

By the summer of 1987, it became clear that searches for nuclear fuel inside Unit 4, with the help of exploring groups, had reached the limit of opportunities. The people were exposed to more danger, and the information gathered grew scant. What did we know by this time?

That almost all the fuel was situated inside Shelter, approximately 180 tons out of the 190 tons of uranium situated in the reactor of Unit 4 before the accident.

During the previous year, analyses of tens of thousands of ground samples were done, samples from near Unit 4 and at the distance of hundreds of kilometers. Planes and helicopters equipped with special instruments explored over the territories of Ukraine, Byelorussia, Russia. Data from foreign colleagues was received. Numerous "cesium spots"—locations of radioactive cesium—were found. And all of that showed that not more than 5% of the fuel—uranium particles with nonflying radionuclides—had been thrown out of the Unit.

We already knew that after the accident, the fuel existed in three different types.

First, in the form of unbroken and destroyed fragments in the active zone: assemblies, rods, uranium tablets, and their parts. Some quantity of those fragments were hurled by the explosion to the area surrounding the Unit—on the buildings' roofs, on the grounds of the ventilation tube. They were gathered partially and thrown back into the ruins or put into containers. Some of those containers were also situated inside Shelter, walled up in concrete. But, of course, all those "visible" fragments were only a small part of what remained in the active zone. It was supposed that the main part lay in the Central Hall under the thousands of tons of various materials thrown from helicopters, "invisible" to us.

The second form of fuel was dust. Or to sound more professional, hot fuel particles (*hot* meaning radioactive). These particles penetrated the surfaces of walls, floors, ceilings, and were in the air. Almost all the premises of Shelter were contaminated. Later, we'll talk about this, an especially "pleasant" fuel modification for us

And the last, lava. Excepting the famous Elephant Leg, lava was discovered in many other places in Shelter, even at the lowest points of Unit 4. It spread via steam relief valves and pipes (fig. 15).

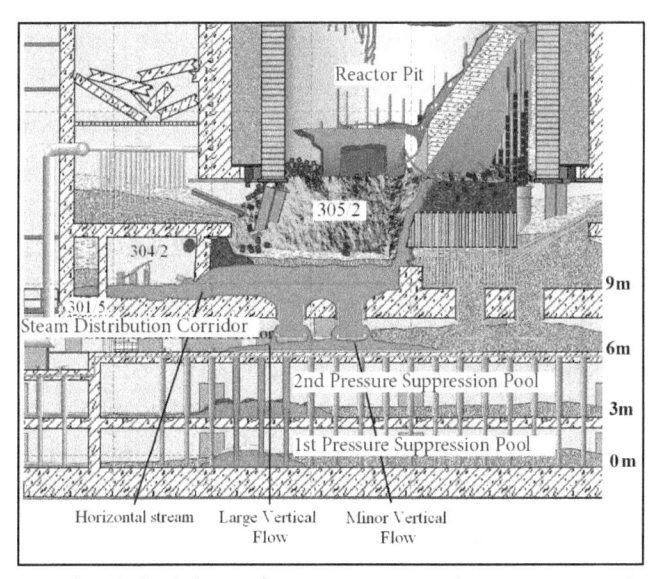

Figure 15. The Shelter's lower fragment crosscut along 46^{+2500} axis. Lava are red. The center of its formation is a room under the reactor—305/2, Concrete that fell into the Shelter's premises during its construction is marked in gray.

Alexender A. Borovoi

Now, about the main results of thermal exploring.

With the help of thermal detectors and the air-stream fixed on buoys, we managed, though roughly, to prove correct the results of external measurements. Really, the overwhelming part of the fuel must be situated inside the Unit.

Thermal measurements made in a room near the Elephant Leg—remember the room in which the photographer was left?—showed that a large amount of fuel (which formed the lava) had penetrated into the room—305/2—right under the reactor. In this room there is a large metallic cross. It serves as support for the entire reactor.

There were a lot of theories about how the fuel got into that room, but as it turned out later, nature was much more inventive than the theorists.

So, our efforts came across immovable obstacles more and more often. The most interesting rooms were inaccessible. And now, not only radiation fields created obstacles for the explorers, but also concrete that got into Shelter and poured through many rooms and corridors.

Only two ways to continue—or not—were left. One: to stop exploring the Unit and wait while, due to the decay of short-living radionuclides, radiation fields were decreased by ten times; and two—to change the strategy and tactics of the exploration in the whole.

The first way wasn't considered seriously. It wasn't possible to leave a radioactive mine with unknown features and a great charge on the ground, when the first two Units were working already and the third was being prepared for starting, and where thousands of people worked day and night.

Almost at every meeting of the Government Commission, we heard reproaches addressed to our Institute that we couldn't find the fuel and answer questions about nuclear hazard.

Only the second way was left.

Having returned to Moscow, I plunged into discussions and talks, which took place mainly on the second floor of the main building, in the office of Academician Belayev. As far as I remember, the owner of this office was the person who first suggested the idea of using boring to get into the inaccessible rooms of the Unit. That is, to bore holes through concrete walls and metallic constructions, and then put proper detectors into the places of supposed fuel congestions.

The further this idea was discussed, the more real and attractive it looked.

Having returned to Chernobyl, I started to work through the tactics of this new attack. I spoke to specialists on reactors, to workers, to geologists. I asked the members of the operative group, who knew the Unit especially well, to come back from Moscow. Nobody refused to help. They came on their holidays, discussed at day and in the night the best places for setting the boring equipment and directions for the first hole-boring. They went to the Unit with me and solved urgent problems. The Institute's laboratories started to work out special detectors that would be fed through the holes.

Every moment, I felt the power of one of the best-in-the-world nuclear centers behind the back of our small Chernobyl group.

In the beginning of October 1987, the first vice minister and the Institute's authorities came to Chernobyl. Discussions of our attack program lasted for the whole day. It was approved in general.

A meeting of the Government Commission was to take

place on the 13th of October. At this meeting, the problem was to be discussed, among other questions.

I still don't know the real reason for everything that happened. But the day before the meeting, all Institute and Ministry authorities left Chernobyl in a great hurry. I got a very short answer to my question as to who would make the report about our future program at the meeting. The answer was: "You!"

Correlating different facts and rumors, I quickly came to the conclusion that a black cat had run between Scherbina and the Ministry authorities. Maybe it didn't have any direct bearing on Chernobyl. This meeting of the Government Commission was a suitable place for the Chairman to punish refractory nuclear workers. And I, to some extent, was left as a hostage.

Of course, nobody wants to be punished in public, and I had no doubts that this punishment was inevitable. The Chairman was a very clever and experienced person. But if a reprimand concerns only your ignorance in the presentation of materials, that is half a trouble. It is a great trouble if a program, having taken so much effort by so many people and promising real progress, is rejected. Not one of my friends would forgive me this, and, most of all, I would never forgive myself.

After a long sleepless night and a gray, empty morning, the day of October 13, 1987, came.

***

Meetings of the Government Commission took place in the hall of a specially built two-story building. Scherbina came in looking gloomy and took his place, pursing his lips. The first report was from the director of the plant. I was always impressed by the talent and business savvy of this man. The Chairman's opinion of him was very high. Nevertheless, the Chairman interrupted the report within ten minutes.

"Who are you? Are you director of the nuclear plant or a beggar on a church porch? What are you reporting about? About electro energy, about plans' fulfillment, about economy of means? No! You are asking for more people and means for deactivation, asking for more equipment, asking, asking without any end! The country is giving everything it can to you. It gives you the last it has. You should have a conscience! This is not a report. I can't adopt it! If tomorrow morning at seven o'clock you won't make a normal report personally, you can't lead the Station, and we'll find somebody else. You are not the last in this world!"

The director grew pale, turned, and walked toward the door, keeping silent and walking unsteadily, like a blind man. Nobody knew, he never confessed that he had a bad heart, and that such a scene could cost him his life.

The next person making a report was sent back to his place in five minutes. It was my turn.

During my long, sleepless night, I invented a method that I thought had a small chance to achieve success and approval of our program. At that moment, those chances seemed to equal zero. Nevertheless, I had no other plan.

I started to speak. About the necessity to clean up and decontaminate some remaining rooms on the west side of the Unit. To settle boring equipment there. To start boring horizontal holes toward the reactor's shaft and in rooms under the reactor. I told about prepared detectors and methods of measurements. Scherbina didn't interrupt me. The time for my inventive trick came. I addressed those present and said that I was just expressing our suggestions on the quantity of the initial holes and their marks, according to which would be bored. There were workers, military, and members of the Government Commission who knew the Unit perfectly well. I would like to listen to their opinions, if they thought we were right to choose the initial bases and the main direction of our attack. Which rooms were more accessible, which were easier to decontaminate. This method was as old as the world—to involve the people present in the discussion, and to make them not critics, but advisors and participants in the program.

The auditorium came to life. Discussion and talks began. Scherbina turned in his chair and added some remarks also.

My performance was finished. I took my place, really amazed, and started to torture a general I knew with questions as I waited in the interval.

Why didn't the Chairman, who had interrupted the people he was kindly disposed to, defeat and toss out of Chernobyl the representative of a hostile team?

Was my report that good?

Had my trick worked successfully?

The general's answer disappointed and cooled me to some extent.

"Yes, the report was good, the idea was not bad and progressive. And the method didn't spoil anything. Everybody was involved in the discussion. And the main thing, the Chairman understood perfectly well that you do not threaten anyone's ego.

"Excuse me for this comparison," he added, "but there was no use to make you a switchman. He will find another place and time to argue with your department."

In any case, the program was adopted.

* * *

In the end of 1987, the Complex Expedition at the Kurchatov Institute was formed in Chernobyl to put this program into practice and to fulfill other works at Shelter (fig. 16).

It included subunits of scientific workers, projectors, builders, assembly workers, and supplying services. A science department was formed of representatives of the biggest Ministry Institutes, and our operative group was its heart. I was appointed manager of this department in 1988.

The idea to form such an organization was quite reasonable. A small—thirty to fifty people—science department worked out tactics and strategy, and fulfilled the task of scientific escort. This department always relied on the main institutes in its work. Other departments of the Complex Expedition fulfilled the outlined plans. The total number of the Expedition at its most intense moments of working was three thousand people.

* * *

By the beginning of 1988, the marked rooms on the west side of the Unit were ready. Hole-boring began.

Figure 16. Shelter in the winter of 1987, at the beginning of the work of the Complex Expedition

5. Seven Days in May

Two Washington journalists, Fletcher Knebel and Charles W. Bailey II, published a book titled *Seven Days in May* in 1962. It quickly became a bestseller, not only in America, but in the whole world.

The tense scenes of the book are laid during just seven days, a week in May. Of course, some of the events are just fruits of the authors' fantasy, but due to their talent, one forgets this and the events seem absolutely true to life.

I read this book with pleasure and remembered it now because for the workers at Shelter, the first seven days in May of 1988 became decisive also. But that time, the events, taking place in real life, acquired to an extent a fantastical character. Every May Day has brought something new, sometimes far from pleasant. The most remarkable events took place on the 1st and the 3rd of May.

* * *

There was an active hole-boring at the Unit.

A portion of the holes were to drill into the thick slab that served as the floor of the under-apparatus room. It was necessary to check whether the fuel, which had penetrated into this room, had started to burn the concrete. That is, whether the damned China Syndrome had started.

Other holes, situated at higher points, were directed to penetrate into the reactor's shaft. We were looking forward to receiving the answers to the following questions: What is left from the active zone? In what condition are those remains? Even a small part of the reactor's assembly of uranium and graphite could present nuclear hazard (fig. 17).

* * *

The first day of May fell on a Sunday. But it wasn't only the weekend, it was one of the greatest holidays—the 1st of May and the 7th of October—celebrated in the Soviet Union.

That was why there were few people inside Shelter by the evening of May 1. There was a group of drillers, working in the lower rooms; people on duty in the room with the control panel; dosimetrists, electricians, and people from the defense service.

The members of our department were gathered at the festive table.

The fact that all troubles always happen on holidays is known perfectly well, and the more serious the trouble is, the later at night it takes place. That's why right at the moment when the fun was at its height, I was called to the telephone. The foreman of the driller's group was calling.

"Some kind of either fog or steam is escaping out of the hole. Its mouth is already hard to see. It will reach the machine soon. What should we do?"

"Lead the people out immediately. Shut all doors and try to seal them hermetically. Wait for me. I'll come soon."

It's easy to say "I'll come soon." I was about fourteen kilometers from the Unit, it was a festive night, and it was impossible to find a car and a sober driver.

But I was prodigiously lucky. One of our drivers had just returned from the tour and hadn't reached the festive table yet.

He returned to his bus without a murmur and we—two other members and I—traveled to the Station along the dark road.

* * *

The drillers were upstairs in the room with the control panel. We went downstairs and came to the doors that led to the corridor. From this corridor, we could reach the room with the boring machines. The doors were slightly closed but were not sealed. Cursing, I walked into the room and shut the door after me. The dust lingering in the air could be perfectly seen, even in the corridor. While I was trying to estimate the situation, there suddenly sounded a voice from behind.

"Permit! Show me your permit!"

The figure of a soldier, pressing a wrongly applied respirator to his mouth, walked toward me out of the fog.

"Why weren't you led out?" I asked. "Did they forget you?"

"No. I can't leave my post."

"And where are the officers?"

"I don't know. They must be coming."

It wasn't difficult to guess where the officers were.

"Can I permit you to leave your post?" I asked.

"But you are a civilian."

"How much time has passed since the fog appeared in the corridor?"

"About five to seven minutes."

"If you stay here for ten minutes more, you won't need to leave this place at all. It will be easier for you to die!" I pronounced the erroneous and cruel words, but I couldn't find any other way at that time.

The soldier ran away.

Alexender A. Borovoi

And we, running by turns into the corridor first and then toward the machines, with the water hose and acting like janitors, splashed water about the rooms, suppressing the fog to some extent.

Fuel dust had again sent us a serious warning.

* * *

So, the water, cooling the boring equipment, had penetrated into the sphere of high temperature. It started to evaporate quickly, decaying the substance and changing it into dust. Streams of air and steam threw this dust back out through the hole.

But for that to happen, something radiating enormous heat must have penetrated into this slab. Fuel? How? By its gradual burning and destroying? This suspicion, connected with the Syndrome, proved correct and was finally confirmed later.

* * *

Holes, coming from above, confirmed one other suspicion the day after. The lower slab of the reactor, having smashed the cross, had dropped down by four meters! Probably, the assembly, the active zone of the reactor, went down with it.

* * *

On the 3rd of May one of the upper holes, passing through concrete walls, sand cover, and the steel walls of the cistern of the water defense, at last reached the reactor's shaft. Considering the assembly had dropped down, its center should have been situated in this place. In the place where the accident was born.

We put a long probe into the hole and tried to determine the borders of the destroyed active zone. The probe went farther and farther without hitting any obstacle. It reached the opposite wall of the cistern at last. The assembly should have been in this cistern, but there was no sign of it.

This happened in the evening. Everybody was so exhausted, so tired after the day, we couldn't realize the importance of this event at once. But, walking to the bus to Chernobyl, we became more and more amazed.

Where was the active zone? Where was the two hundred tons of uranium, the immense quantity of graphite?

During the next days, a second hole was bored near the first one at the same height, at all maximum possible speed. Powerful searchlights were put into the reactor's shaft through this second hole. A special periscope was put into the shaft through the first hole.

The shaft turned out to be practically empty!

Those seven days in May ended with this surprising event.

But our sufferings were not finished yet.

First, a sigh of relief gushed out of the chest of every member of the Complex Expedition.

The most hazardous—considering spontaneous nuclear reaction—uranium-graphite assembly had stopped existing. But after the sigh of relief, a sad sigh sounded. We still had to find the fuel that had disappeared.

This research is still being done. The various dramatic and comic situations connected with that search are beyond the frame of this small book.

I would like to tell the following, though. Already in the

Alexender A. Borovoi

spring of 1989, it was reported to the Government Commission that all of the fuel-containing masses discovered by this time were nuclear safe at the moment.

The Final Chapter

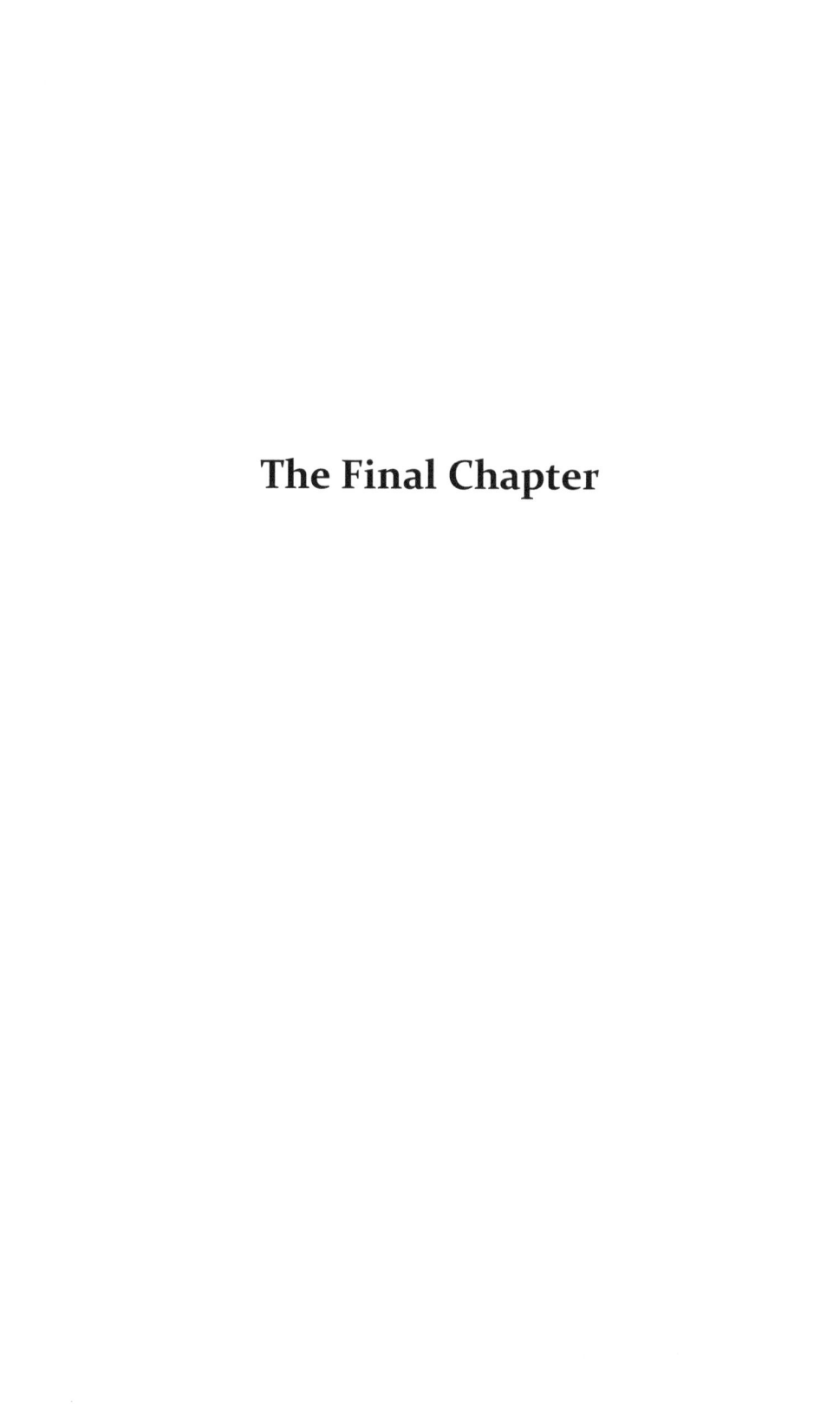

Wheels are clattering. Train. Approximately once a month, I go by the route Moscow-Kiev-Chernobyl, and then come back to Moscow in twenty days. During these first eight years, there have been about 150 such tours, more than 2000 hours in the trains. I am looking out the window, thinking. When I go to Chernobyl, I think about my work. When I head back to Moscow, I think about seeing my wife, sons, and grandchildren.

And now all my thoughts are devoted to my book. I was going to write no more than fifty pages, but I was carried away by the book, and now the number is coming inevitably to one hundred. I have very little time. I am to fly to the USA in four days. Also, a translation into English must be done. (Julya, my daughter-in-law, is working on it.)

But first of all, I must read everything written in Chernobyl to my main reader, my wife. During the decades of our joint life, she must have listened to several thousand pages. Everything I have ever written, excepting entirely scientific articles.

I can't imagine the future readers very well.

How will they perceive these pieces of Chernobyl life?

I don't know.

* * *

In 1991, Edward Briffa, a BBC director, created a film—*Inside Chernobyl's Sarcophagus*—about the people working inside Shelter. There is an episode in the film when some members of the Kurchatov Institute are having their dinner and talking about the things that prevent them from doing their work at the Unit. Everybody agrees that it is not radiation but an invincible bureaucracy of different ranks. Those who are called to ensure the work, and those who apply the brakes to it.

One of the members, who saved the photographer near the Elephant Leg, gives examples of our poor life at Shelter. There is a shortage of special clothes. Sometimes there are not even any socks.

When we see the finished film, we run the bureaucracy down hopelessly once again, but we don't attach great importance to the socks.

* * *

This film was released successfully on TV in England, France, and the United States. In spite of "Great Perestroika," it wasn't seen in Russia and Ukraine.

* * *

One morning, my secretary called me to Shelter and said that there was a parcel from Scotland addressed to me, very big and suspiciously light. The first thing I did in the evening was to rush to open this parcel. Inside was a package, and then another one inside that, and at last ... a dozen nice hand-knit woolen socks. I was slightly shocked, and remained in this condition until I found a short message.

A married couple from Scotland wrote that they saw the film and liked it very much. They understood from the film that the Kurchatovers, working in difficult conditions, didn't have the most necessary things. Unfortunately, this couple wasn't rich. They were pensioners. Mary, the wife, earned extra money by knitting. And she knitted those socks for us with pleasure, because they were absolutely necessary in Russia, where it was very cold.

At the next meeting of our group, I stood up, showed the parcel to everybody, and said, "From this moment, the highest reward for professionalism in work will be a pair of socks, knitted by a Scottish woman."

And I rewarded the first pair to one of our best workers.

A second parcel with socks came in a week from Canada. Then a third, and a fourth. The only foreign country that hasn't sent socks yet is Australia. No doubt, this parcel is still on its way.

* * *

The train is coming to Moscow.

The time given to me is up.

I am glancing through the pages, faces and events flashing. The old woman is making the sign of the cross over me ...

People of the evicted village are waiting silently for the verdict ...

The soldier is coming to me out of radioactive fog, pressing the respirator to his face with his hand ...

A woman in Scotland is bending over her knitting ...

On the platform, in the rain, my wife is standing.

Thank you for everything, and good-bye!

Conclusion—2017

My Chernobyl is focused on the first years after the accident. In those years, we succeeded in creating "Shelter," which is known in the press as the Sarcophagus. Shelter enclosed the destroyed Unit 4 and defined where to look for the missing nuclear fuel. We needed to understand whether it constituted further danger, and to plan ways in which this danger could be prevented, controlled, or eliminated.

While it was a great amount of work, unfortunately, it was only a part of what can be considered a complete elimination of the consequences of the accident.

What occurred in the next years?

By the end of 1989, scientists could survey in detail the majority of the rooms within Shelter. They found out not only about the high collective dose received by the builders, but also about the basic shortcomings of Shelter that were the result of the record-breaking quickness of its creation.

The first of the large shortcomings of Shelter was the enormous number of cracks. Because of the huge radiation fields, it had been impossible to implement the established designs to achieve the fewest cracks and to weld seams closed. As a result, the total area of cracks in the roof and walls equaled about 1000 square meters. This meant that radioactive dust could get out of Shelter, and water from rains and snow could get inside.

The second shortcoming was the uncertain durability of the old building's structural frame on which the new structure of Shelter leaned. These supports had been weakened by the explosion and fire. It was not possible to measure their strength or durability. In the case of a strong earthquake, which happens in this area once every one hundred to two hundred years, nobody could guarantee it would not collapse.

Therefore, in 1989, S. T. Belyaev—also of the Kurchatov Institute—and I created a concept to transform Shelter to make it completely, ecologically safe. The main point of our concept: construct another tight cover (New Safe Confinement) over the existing Shelter, which would last many decades and protect the external environment from radioactive emissions. At the same time, it would protect Shelter from any external influences—an earthquake, a tornado, etc. This cover would allow the development of further technologies, which might make it safe to take, and then to bury, radioactive materials and nuclear fuel.

The concept was supported in Ukraine. Since 1991, the Chernobyl Nuclear Power Plant has been under that country's jurisdiction. The Ukrainian government decided to hold an international competition for Shelter's transformation to an ecologically safe system.

On June 17, 1993, the competition was complete. Elaboration of the strategy for creating a new safe containment was the main result. It was obvious this strategy would require enormous amounts of materials. It was also necessary to address the need for international aid. The first step in this direction was taken at the end of 1993.

In December 1993, the Vice President of the United States, Albert Gore, paid an official visit to Russia. During one of his meetings, the president of the Kurchatov Institute, E. Velikhov, told him about the problems with Shelter. At the vice president's request, Velikhov gave him a memorandum (fig. 16) that contained a request for help with the transformation of Shelter.

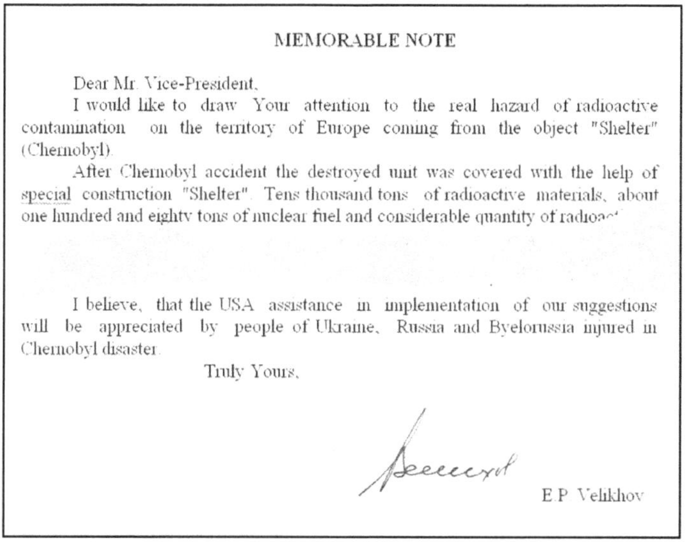

> **MEMORABLE NOTE**
>
> Dear Mr. Vice-President,
> I would like to draw Your attention to the real hazard of radioactive contamination on the territory of Europe coming from the object "Shelter" (Chernobyl).
> After Chernobyl accident the destroyed unit was covered with the help of special construction "Shelter". Tens thousand tons of radioactive materials, about one hundred and eighty tons of nuclear fuel and considerable quantity of radioa~~
>
> I believe, that the USA assistance in implementation of our suggestions will be appreciated by people of Ukraine, Russia and Byelorussia injured in Chernobyl disaster.
> Truly Yours,
>
> E.P. Velikhov

Figure 16. The first and last pages of a memorandum about the need for transformation of Shelter, as sent to Vice President Al Gore.

After some time, I was sent to Washington as the representative of the Kurchatov Institute. Together with Gary Dunbar, at that time a vice president of LATA (Los Alamos Technical Associates), I described in detail the condition of Shelter at meetings in the White House, the State Department, and with the Nuclear Regulatory Commission (fig. 17). The possibilities of the United States participating in the transformation of Shelter, and in the creation of special international funding to finance the work, were discussed.

Alexender A. Borovoi

Figure 17. Alexander Borovoi, Boris Prister, Senator Joseph Lieberman, and Alex Stolyarov in the Senator's office in Washington. Photo Credit: Gary Dunbar

The request stated in the memorandum was received with understanding and support. It was the first practical step on the way to realization of the suggested strategy. I must add that on the Russian side, they sought to draw the attention of the international public to the question of the safety of Shelter. But certainly, the leading role in seeking a solution to the problem of transforming Shelter was played by the consistent and persistent policy of the President of Ukraine and the Ukrainian government.

Several years passed before the necessary funds were raised.

In 1997, at a meeting of the Group of Seven (Canada, France, Germany, Italy, the United Kingdom, and the United States—Russia was a guest), the Shelter Implementation Plan (SIP) was accepted. This plan defined a number of the actions needed for Shelter's transformation to an ecologically safe state.

That same year in New York, the conference of the donor countries that created the Chernobyl Fund—Ukrytiye—took place. Management of the fund was entrusted to the European Bank for Reconstruction and Development (EBRD). The term for completing the SIP was determined to be eight to nine years. The cost of all the work was estimated at $758 million.

Part of the work was to construct near Shelter, in a place where there were acceptable radiation fields, a huge arch.

Then, on special rails, this arch would be pulled over Shelter and the end closed up (see fig. 18).

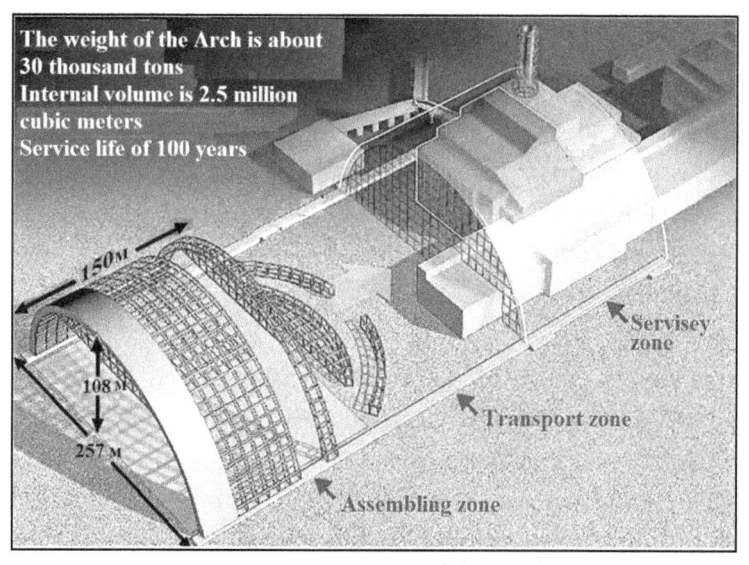

Figure 18. Concept of the arch.

Unfortunately, as often happens, it was not possible to correctly estimate all the difficulties that would occur. The original plan wasn't successful, and the work had to be reorganized.

As a result, only by 2017 was decisive success with the SIP realized: the built metal arch (fig. 19) was pulled over the existing Shelter and the end was closed by special designs.

Alexender A. Borovoi

Figure 19. The arch enclosing Shelter, 2017

It is necessary to say that so far, the cost for construction has exceeded one billion dollars. EBRD states on their website that the total cost was $2.3 billion.

Now, the next stage of transformation—the dismantling, under the protection of the arch, of the most dangerous, damaged structural elements and contaminated radioactive materials and nuclear fuel from the destroyed Unit 4, and their final burial—will begin.

There are also new difficulties. Extraction of the destroyed fuel: this is an operation that has not been practiced anywhere before, and for which there are no previous examples.

However, the experts working at the platform of the CNPP had sufficient time to organize this work. By all current estimates, the new confinement will ensure full safety for one hundred years.

* * *

For these past years I have often heard the question: If Shelter doesn't now threaten Europe or America, why are dozens of countries providing large sums of money for more work to increase its safety?

I answer this question in the following manner:

- because of concern for the lives of the people now working at the CNPP, in the Chernobyl area, and living nearby in Ukraine and neighboring countries;

- and the need to demonstrate that mankind has contained "The Chernobyl Syndrome."

Afterword

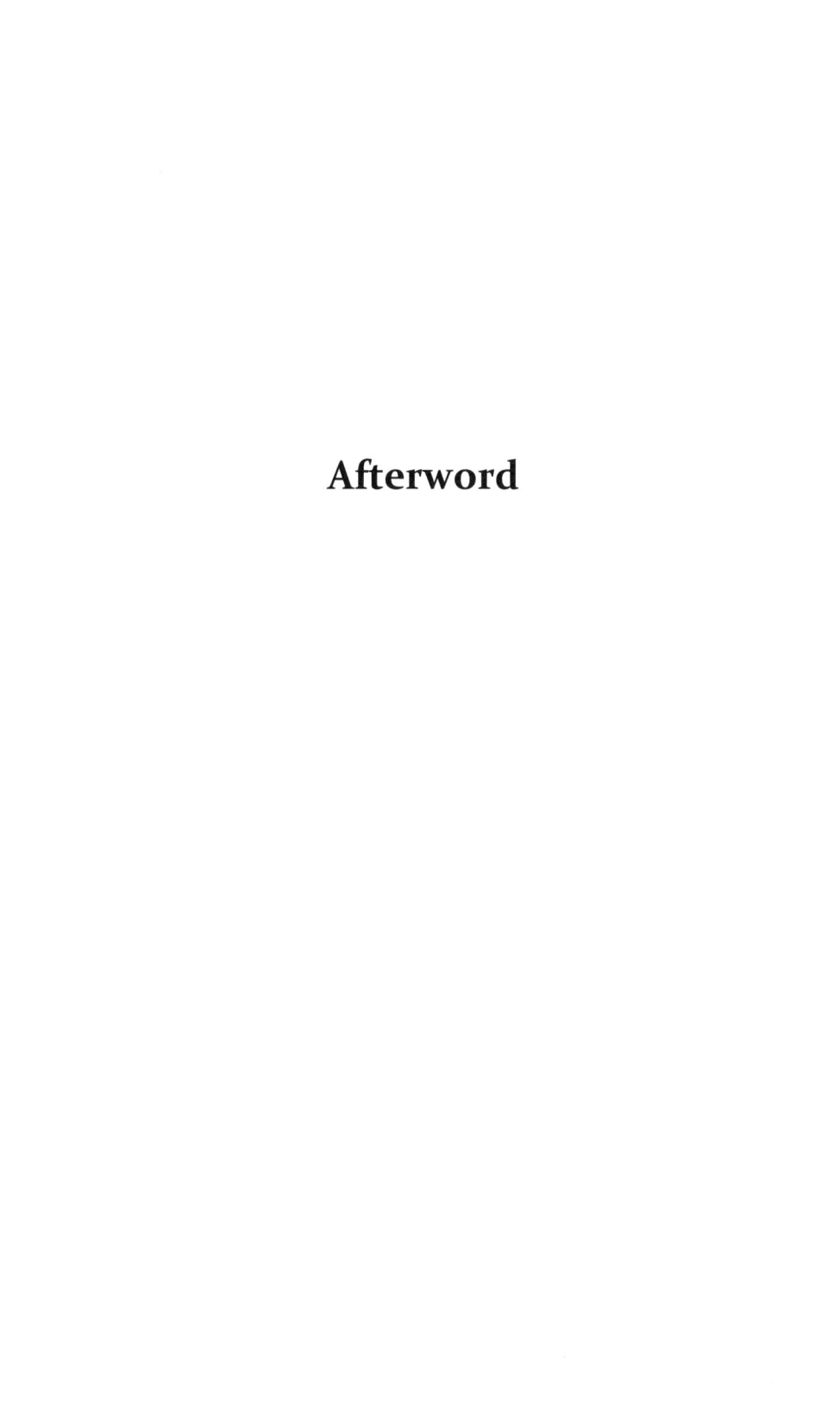

In 2016, Cesium 137 contamination spread by the Chernobyl accident reached its half-life, and the New Safe Confinement (NSC) was rolled into place, beginning its one-hundred-year life of containing the radioactive remains of Chernobyl's Unit 4 and the sarcophagus. A structure that cost $2.3 billion. Perhaps the most obvious lessons are that accidents with nuclear energy take a long time to resolve and cost a great deal of money. A subtle but possibly even more important lesson is that unanticipated catastrophes, for which we have no significant recognition or planning, ignite well-meant yet ineffective, costly, and potentially lethal initial phases.

Our planet faces an increasing number of potential future catastrophes for which no meaningful plans of response exist. Indeed, in some cases, political leadership denies the potential or reality of catastrophe. Consider that it required more than 100,000 years for the total human population on Earth to reach one billion people. Our population is now more than 7.5 billion, and is projected to exceed 11 billion in less than 300 years after that first one-billion milestone was achieved. Combine population growth with specie extinctions; reductions in the supply of potable water and in crop lands; increasing (and increasingly) violent and destructive weather; and, of course, the human violence that erupts from our complex, worldwide cultural mix, and you can glimpse the fragility of our situation. It is possible that a city with ten

Alexender A. Borovoi

million or more residents could easily be destroyed in less than one hour by a single event, either natural or manmade.

Borovoi, and others like him, having confronted one of the worst manmade catastrophes of our modern age, have set a standard for human behavior that sees through the panic, confusion, and misguided responses that catastrophes spawn, and helps all of us survive.

—Gary Dunbar

About the Author

Alexander A. Borovoi was born in Moscow and has lived there all his life, including the twenty-three years that he commuted to Chernobyl. He is a family man, and he and his wife Tamila have sons and daughters-in-law, grandchildren, and great-grandchildren.

He graduated from the Moscow Engineering Physical University in 1962 and entered the Kurchatov Institute as a young engineer. He progressed to Senior Research Associate, and then to Candidate, and finally to Doctor of Nuclear Physics. He collaborated and exchanged ideas with the "great generation"—A.P. Alexandrov, S.T. Belyaev, I.K. Kikoin, Y.A. Smorodinsky, G.N. Flerov, and many others. Borovoi established the neutrino physics laboratory at the second reactor of the Rivne Nuclear Power Plant, where he developed the detector for neutrino particles.

The Chernobyl accident in 1986 pulled Borovoi and thousands of others into a whirlpool of events. His focus for twenty-three years was the reduction and elimination of the consequences of the accident. He continues that work today at the Kurchatov Institute.

In addition to his Russian academic diplomas, he received the award "For Courage" and the State award, and a rank of the "honored worker in science and technology." In August 2001, *U.S. News and World Report* included Borovoi in its list of twenty living "real heroes." The Russian literary magazine *New World* identified his book, *My Chernobyl*, as the best work in journalism published in 1996.

CPSIA information can be obtained
at www.ICGtesting.com
Printed in the USA
BVHW071345010719
552379BV00023B/1948/P

9 781944 393724